HIEROGLYPHS FOR TRAVELERS

By Thomas F. Mudloff and Ronald E. Fellows

This book is provided as a field guide to help you recognize and identify the names of the pharaohs, their queens, their nobles, and their gods as you visit the monuments, tombs, and temples of ancient Egypt. Although the complete study of hieroglyphic writing is the work of a lifetime, you will learn enough here to interpret the names of some of the more important rulers and to recognize certain sign groups and magical funerary formulas.

Cover: Seti I and his young son Ramesses II worship the cartouche names of their ancestors on the King Table at the Temple of Abydos. *By Daniel Loeillet*

Back cover: The underside of a lintel at Medinet Habu Photo by Paul Kloppenborg.

HiEROGLYPHS for TRAVELERS

Hieroglyphs for Travelers
What do those little pictures mean?

by Thomas F. Mudloff and Ronald E. Fellows

Published by R.E. Fellows Publishing
2014 Siegle Drive
Lemon Grove, CA 91945 USA
(619) 465-3841

ISBN 0-939968-02-9
Library of Congress Card Number: 99-091135
Printed in the United States of America

Dedications

Dedicated to my Best Buddy,
Nora Robertson.
Nora loved Egypt, and Egypt loved Nora
- Ron

For Judy: A true Master of Secrets.
For her support and encouragement.
-Tom

HIEROGLYPHS FOR TRAVELERS

Table of Contents

Now, Read the Names of the Kings, their Queens, their Nobles, and their Gods— Site by Site

Appendix

There is much variation in the translation of hieroglyphic writing into English words. An example is the name of the god *Imn* which may be written: Amon, Amen, Amun or Amoun. Then too, the classical Greek authors renamed the pharaohs into Greek: Khufu, Khafre and Menkaura became Cheops, Chephren and Mycerinus. This book will retain the original Egyptian names. Since the scribes of Egypt, like the Arabs and Hebrews, used no vowels, Egyptologists have sprinkled E's where needed in order to pronounce the words. The triliteral sign ⌂ for *htp* then , may be read as hetep or hotep.

Rising above the Valley of the Kings is a natural pyramid that must have symbolized the earlier royal burials to the Egyptians. At first, sacred to the goddess Hathor, it was later associated with Meretseger, "She who loves silence."

Preface: An Ancient Language Unlocked

Much can be said about the language of the ancient Egyptians, and indeed has been said. There are any number of books in print on the subject and these range from more intense studies of the language, like Sir Alan Gardiner's "Egyptian Grammar", to others which are less intense. Most of these fall into the pedagogical category of "grammar translation", meaning, that the student works from a basis of spoon-fed grammar lessons and a vocabulary that is presented lesson by lesson. The grammar is taught without regard to meaningful context. Little attention is paid to the idea of language in its cultural background with many of the lessons and examples presented in a disassociated nature that have no basis in real usage. The learning climate is one of the challenges being sufficient reward for months of drill and practice. Emphasis is always on an analysis of the rules.

This type of an approach, i.e. theory of education in the field, has come under attack by educators and in pedagogical thinking generally, in recent years. ***Thus, one of the aims of this book is to present an introduction to this ancient language, in a form that can be seen within the cultural context and in an authentic way.***

The new student should not feel put off by the array of seeming contradictions in the language, for with patience and a bit of effort, an amazing world will open to the explorer. The language of ancient Egypt is magic, and when you, the traveler, unlock its secrets, you will not only become the magician, but will also be a participant in the on-going journey to keep alive the words of those who lived so many centuries before us. They had but one wish, that their names live forever. When you speak their language and utter their names, their wish is fulfilled and you help bridge the centuries to join with them and their ancient wisdom.

An old Egyptian woman. Does she recall the language of the ancients?

Cartouche: The Sun's Circuit. The circle, sacred in societies throughout the world, expresses the idea of eternity; no beginning, no end. In ancient Egypt the cartouche, that elongated circular device that surrounds pharaohs' names and represents the circuit of the sun, grew out of this concept. The hieroglyphs for *encircle*, $\bigcirc$ $\bigcirc$, also have the connotation of protection. As in ancient magical practices, to encircle something is to protect it and so the royal nomen and prenomen are the kings' name written across the space of all that the sun encircles, or eternity and the protection thus afforded. The name "cartouche" is modern, given the symbol by the French at the time of Napoleon. In French, the term denotes gun cartridge or an ornamental frame. Look for this symbol carried in the claws of the falcon form of Horus and the various vulture goddesses.

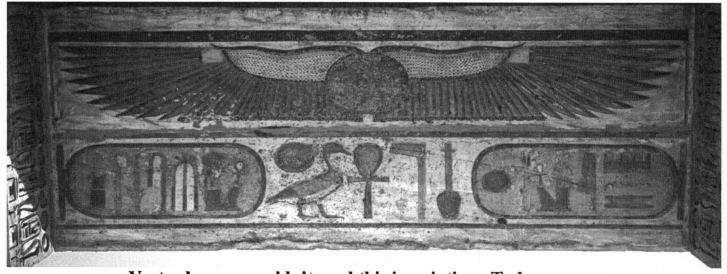

Yesterday you couldn't read this inscription. Today you can.

Introduction: The Magic that is Ancient Egypt

Here in Egypt, there is magic. You will find it, and its mystery will surround you.

In order to understand magic in Ancient Egypt we must first understand the nature of how the ancients viewed this force and what its appropriate use was in the world order. It must first be realized that our modern view of the subject, that of implied trickery or deceit is not the view taken by the ancients. Hans Betz, in *The Greek Magical Papyri in Translation* gives a good definition of our modern view when he states that magic is nothing more than *"the idea that something can be done about those things for which we know nothing can be done."*

This characterization will not work for the ancient Egyptians. In their society, magic was a normal aspect of daily life and was the divine force used by the gods themselves to keep world order or Ma'at. As such, there was never any indication of disapproval of magic itself. Magic is seen in the ancient writings as a personification of the creator god himself. Egyptian theology tells us that Atum, the creator-god, created his eldest son Shu by means of his creative energy or magical strength. This supernatural or even occult power of Atum may be seen as the emanation or hypostasis of a unique god called Heka, or Magician. As such, this god may be accounted as the oldest son of the creator god. This force was manifested at the time of creation and was available to be taped into by certain individuals such as priests.

The Magician is counted as one of the seven ba's or external manifestations of Re (Atum) and one of his fourteen ka's or essential forms. He is not only the ka and ba of Re but he is also, according to Egyptian theology, the *name* of Re.

This leads us to another point worth mentioning in this regard. The name of something was thought to contain the essence of that particular object, whether it is as simple as a rock or complex as a person, it has a position no less than that of the ka. The Egyptians looked to the name as one of the seven expressed aspects of a person's soul with all the significance that implies. The papyrus Bremmer-Rhind tells us that Re, while doing the work of creation, says, "My name is Magician." Further, stories tell us of the divine gift of magic made by the gods to man, and that it is entirely proper for our use upon earth. Such a story is the *Instruction Addressed to King Merikare* of Ninth/Tenth Dynasty date. This story which can be classified essentially as a Wisdom Text gives advice from a dead king to his son, the new king. It is clearly stated that god has made (for man) magic as weapons to ward off the blow of events.

Magic itself was not seen as either good or evil, only the ends to which it was put would determine this. White magic, which is perhaps a modern term that we use and not necessarily reflective of ancient Egyptian thought, would be used for healing and comfort. Sorcery, or black magic, was regarded as evil because of its social effects. It is interesting to note, however, that the methods employed are the same in either case. Many of the same utterances or spells that could be used for socially unacceptable purposes, and so falling under the heading of sorcery, were also used in the daily rituals in the temples throughout Egypt as part of the liturgy. The Papyrus Lee, of the New Kingdom period, tells us about a famous *Harem Conspiracy* in which the various scrolls which were, in fact, in the library of king Ramesses III and used for what might be termed practical theology, were used to cast spells against the pharaoh himself! Magic, when used against the enemies of the state or for healing purposes, was deemed completely acceptable. When this same magic was used against the king, it was sorcery and punishable by death!

Magic, as a functioning part of state ritual regarding kingly succession, can be seen in the tomb of Tutankhamun. Here, on the north wall, we see the image of the deceased king Tutankhamun having the magical ritual known as the *Opening of the Mouth* performed on him by the next pharaoh, Ay, wearing a leopard skin of a setem-priest (a priest of high rank). This was a complex set of rituals designed to restore life to a non-living thing such as a statue, an image of a god or human, or a mummy. The apex of the ceremony was reached, as shown here, when the mouth, ears, and eyes of the mummy were touched, i.e. opened, with ritual implements including the small adze tipped with iron or flint as we see in this scene.

Both the mummiform king Tutankhamon and the new king Ay are seen to have their names enclosed in a cartouche. On the left before the dead king's face we read right to left and top to bottom *"The good god, lord of the Two Lands, the lord appearing in Thebes, the king of Upper and Lower Egypt, Neb-Kheperu-Re, son of Re, Tut-Ankh-Amon, Heka-iunu-shema."* Below the two cartouches read *"given life forever."*

In front of the face of king Ay on the right and reading left to right, top to bottom, *"The good god, lord of the Two Lands, lord of ceremonies, the king of Upper and Lower Egypt, Kheperu Re, son of Re, Ay, gods father (it-netjer), given life like Re forever and ever."*

Looking down the wall to the left is seen Tutankhamon before the goddess Nut, identified above her head as *"Nut, Lady of Heaven, Mistress of the gods, she performs nyny (a ceremony) for the one born to her, she gives health and life to your nostril, may you live forever!"*

Next to this scene observe Osiris greeting Tutankhamon and his ka. Reading right to left before the face of Osiris *"Osiris, Foremost of the West, the great god."* Above the king and reading left to right, top to bottom: *"The good god, lord of the Two Lands, lord of appearance, Neb-Kheperu-Re, given life forever and ever".* Above the royal ka, indicated by the up-raised arms on his head read left to right, top to bottom, *"King's ka, lord of the tomb (sarcophagus)."*

You will read all this later.

4

Ancient Egyptian Books of the Afterlife

One of the most interesting developments of the New Kingdom period in Egypt is the emergence of the various so-called *Books* that attempted to chart the world of the beyond. Many are familiar with the *Book of the Dead* but it should be pointed out that this is but one of a series of such works that have survived on either tomb walls or in papyri. Most of these books were derived from the earlier Pyramid Texts that were employed by the kings of the 5th and 6th dynasties. Each of these however developed it's own unique form. The names we know them by are all of modern extraction and do not necessarily reflect their original designations. While no single tomb included all these texts, many show various *chapters* that were chosen by the tomb owners or the artist.

The main theme of these books is that life and death is a continuous process; life endures death and in death there is new life or rebirth. The personification of this process is through two main divinities of ancient Egypt. The sun god Re, the living god who descends into the realm of death every evening and the god of the dead, Osiris, who is transformed by the presence of Re in the underworld. The realm of the dead is identified in these compositions as the body of Osiris. All of these *books* use mythological allusions as a special language to explain the stages in the process of death and regeneration.

It should be understood that the process itself is always the same, but the differentiating element is the varying points of view expressed in the different compositions. At times the stress is placed upon the actual process of transformation of the dead body of the sun god into a new living form. At others, the main theme is one of listing recitations or spells that will successfully allow the deceased to pass unhindered to the Fields of the Blessed. In chapter 17 of the Book of the Dead the deceased is identified with Osiris *" I am yesterday, I know the morrow"* with Egyptian commentary *"What is this? Osiris is yesterday, Re is tomorrow"* (The Egyptian Book of the Dead, The Papyrus of Ani, R.O. Faulkner, 1994).

The sun is the power that brings Osiris and the deceased, who is identified with him, to life again. In the royal books it is the Osiris-king who is revivified anew each dawn and is risen as Re from the realm of the night. From this we understand that Osiris is not merely the Lord of the Am-Duat (underworld) but also the prototype of resurrection and a symbol of life everlasting. Though the sun god is the creator of the world, he is nevertheless borne every day by the sky goddess Nut and swallowed by her every evening. The main feature of all these compositions is the progression of the dead sun god through the realm of darkness, the Duat, the body of his mother Nut as the night sky. Here then is one of the major enigmas of Egyptian religion; the underworld is contained in the body of the sky goddess.

Important Books of the Afterlife

Book of the Dead: Probably the best known of these compositions, it is found in both royal and commoner tombs alike. The Egyptians called the composition *The Book of Going Forth by Day* and various *chapters* can be seen on the walls of some tombs. This is actually a collection of spells of a magical nature, many of which are derived from the earlier Coffin and Pyramid Texts.

The AmDuat: Known by the name *That Which is in the Underworld,* was called *The Book of the Secret Chamber* by the Egyptians. It is the earliest work that attempts to chart the sun god's journey through the 12 divisions of the underworld, which correspond to the 12 hours of the night. Look for good copies of this on the walls in the tombs of Tuthmosis III and Amonhotep II.

Book of Gates: This is a late 18th dynasty work and appears on the walls in the burial chamber and first pillared hall in later tombs. The name is in reference to the 12 gates that separate the hours of the night. Each gate had its own name with a guardian serpent spitting fire. The sun god is seen traveling in a boat accompanied by Sia (mind or perception) and Heka (magic).

One of the most complete versions is in the tomb of Ramesses VI, but the tomb of Ramesses I has some good and well preserved scenes. Parts may also be seen in some private tombs.

Book of Caverns: Here the underworld is seen as a series of pits and caves over which the sun god passes. Afterlife reward and punishment is the focus here and the ultimate destruction of the enemies of the sun god. The scenes are most usually placed in the upper parts of royal tombs of the 20th dynasty. The most complete are in the tomb of Ramesses VI, but again others will show parts of it, such as the tombs of Ramesses IV and IX.

Litany of Re: With its origins in the 18th dynasty, this composition acclaims the sun god Re in 75 different forms. Additionally, it praises the king in his union with the sun god and other deities. Look for it on the pillars in the burial chamber in the tomb of Tuthmosis III and at the entrance of most tombs after Sety I.

Book of the Heavens: This composition is of New Kingdom date and can be seen in a number of Ramesside burial chambers. The intent is to describe the sun's passage through the heavens. The better known of this group are the Book of the Day, the Book of the Night, and the Divine Cow. The most famous of these is to be found in the tomb of Ramesses VI on the ceiling of the burial chamber and lower passages showing parts of the Book of Day and Book of Night. This can also be viewed in the burial chamber of Ramesses IX. Look for the sun as a dark red disc passing through the body of the sky goddess Nut.

The Arrangement of Hieroglyphs: Beauty or Spelling

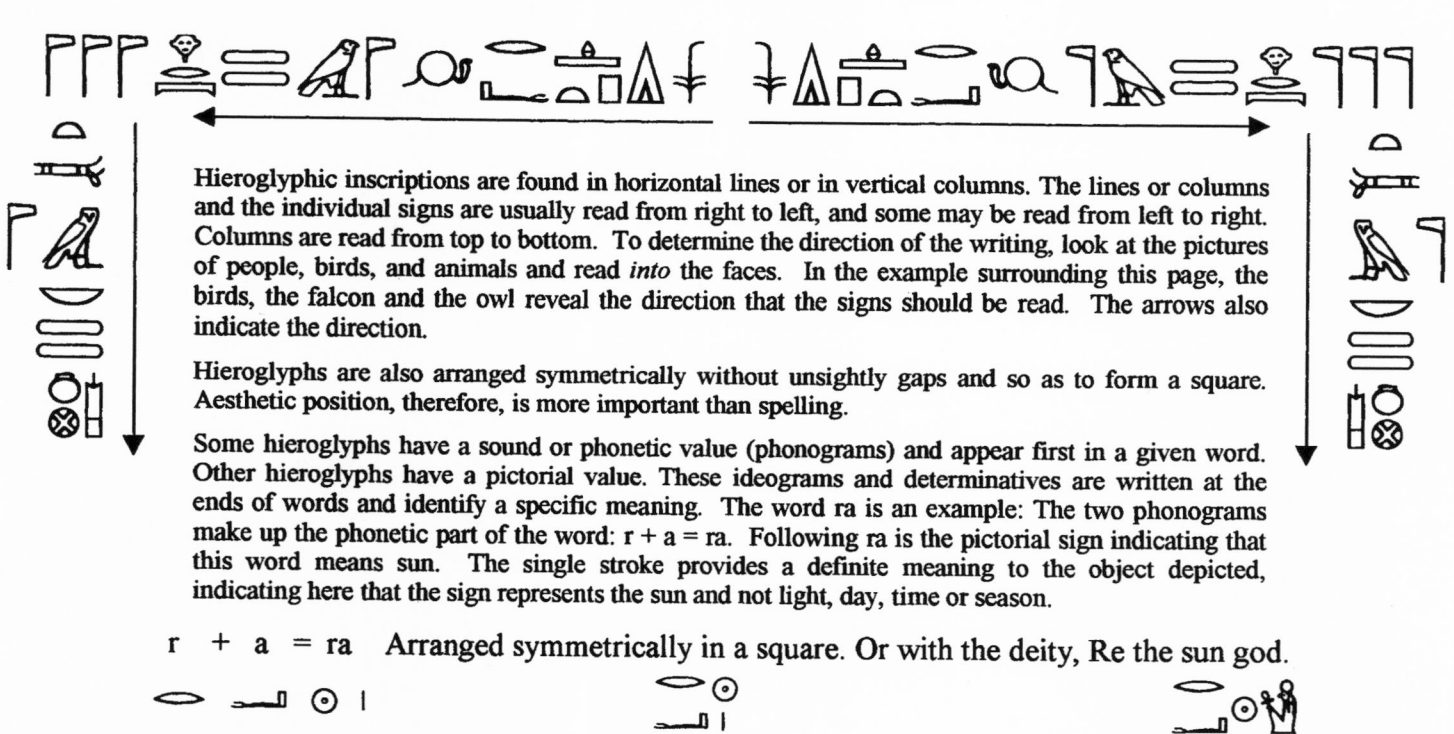

Hieroglyphic inscriptions are found in horizontal lines or in vertical columns. The lines or columns and the individual signs are usually read from right to left, and some may be read from left to right. Columns are read from top to bottom. To determine the direction of the writing, look at the pictures of people, birds, and animals and read *into* the faces. In the example surrounding this page, the birds, the falcon and the owl reveal the direction that the signs should be read. The arrows also indicate the direction.

Hieroglyphs are also arranged symmetrically without unsightly gaps and so as to form a square. Aesthetic position, therefore, is more important than spelling.

Some hieroglyphs have a sound or phonetic value (phonograms) and appear first in a given word. Other hieroglyphs have a pictorial value. These ideograms and determinatives are written at the ends of words and identify a specific meaning. The word ra is an example: The two phonograms make up the phonetic part of the word: r + a = ra. Following ra is the pictorial sign indicating that this word means sun. The single stroke provides a definite meaning to the object depicted, indicating here that the sign represents the sun and not light, day, time or season.

r + a = ra   Arranged symmetrically in a square. Or with the deity, Re the sun god.

The Five Royal Names of the Pharaohs

From the Middle Kingdom, the 11th and 12th Dynasties, the king was given a unique combination of five names. The first was his actual birth name, the other four were conferred on him at his enthronement.

Birth Name
Son of Re

Throne Name
King of Upper
and Lower Egypt

Golden Horus Name
Golden Horus

Nebti Name
He of the Two Ladies

Horus Name
Horus

In the example here, the five names of Tuthmosis III are shown. Read the glyphs from right to left. The sign for the Two Ladies represent the unification of Upper and Lower Egypt. Generally, only the Birth Name and the Throne name are found on statues and monuments. These will be the focus of this book.

The Serekh is a device that represented a palace façade and contained the first and oldest of the kings five part titulary; that of the Horus name. It signifies that the king is the incarnation of Horus and is the one who lives in the palace.

Horus Name
Strong bull, arising in Thebes

Nebti Name
Two Ladies, enduring of kingship, like Re in heaven.

Golden Horus Name
Horus of gold, Powerful of strength, holy of diadems (or risings).

Throne Name
King of upper and Lower Egypt, Menkheperre, established in the form of Re.

Birth Name
Son of Re, Tuthmosis [Thoth is born] beautiful of form.

Distinctive Features of Hieroglyphic Writing

Phonetic Complements: Biliteral and Triliteral (two or three letter) signs are often complemented with one or two monoliteral (one letter) signs that repeat the whole or part of the sound value. Often only the last consonantal sound of a multi-letter sign is repeated, but multiple additions are not uncommon. The phonetic complement is not pronounced and not transliterated.

Signs may be written:

mn or mn - ankh or ankh - nefer or nefer - hetep or hetep

Phonetic complements indicate that the sign is a phonogram (sound sign) and not an idiogram.

Honorific Transposition

Signs indicating king or god and the names of specific kings or gods often appear before the sign for other words that were actually pronounced first.

Examples: Re like   (or)   Amon   Beloved

Written:
Re Like   (or)   Amon   Beloved

But pronounced:
Like Re   Beloved of Amon

Geometric Signs and Numerals

Singular	Plural or W	1	2	3	4	5	6

10	100	1,000	10,000	100,000	1,000,000

Now read this number.
Read from the left.

The Egyptian Dating System

The Egyptian calendar was divided into 12 months of thirty days each. Each year ended with five extra days–called *epagomenal* days: a time for celebration. The Egyptians knew that their year was six hours shorter than the solar year and under Greek rule corrected the discrepancy when they added one day every four years. The Egyptian year consisted of three seasons of four months each whose names referred to agricultural activity: the inundation season (*Achet*), the summer (*Sjemoe*), and the winter (*Peret*). From the Middle Kingdom, the counting of years began again from the year one with the reign of each new ruler.

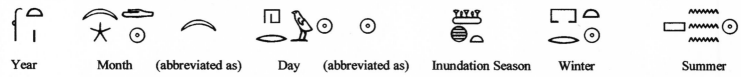

| Year | Month | (abbreviated as) | Day | (abbreviated as) | Inundation Season | Winter | Summer |

This hieroglyph usually indicates a regnal year.

Now you can read the following:

Twenty second regnal year, 2ᵈ month of winter, 23ʳᵈ day, under the majesty of the king of Upper and Lower Egypt, Tuthmosis III

You will find other hieroglyphic dating on Merenptah's Victory stele in the Cairo Museum, Hall 13, and also the Annals of Tuthmosis III at Karnak, (behind the sixth pylon along the main axis, just before the sanctuary), shows a series of dates.

10

Logograms: Ideograms and Determinatives

The hieroglyphic writing system began with ideograms, pictorial signs that represented entire words or a single sound. The picture stood for what it depicted. A chair was a chair; a fish was a fish.

Determinatives were developed to designate a specific purpose to words that may have a variety of meanings. Here is how determinatives clarify the meaning of words.

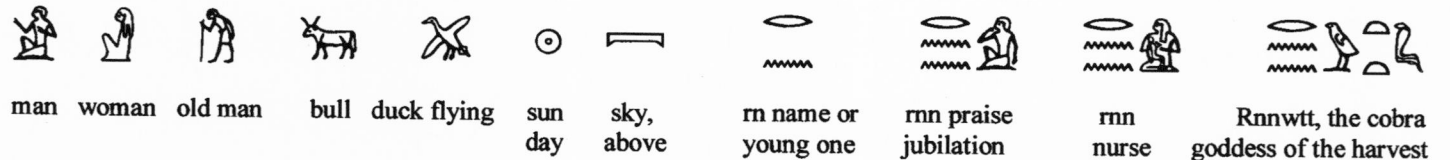

| man | woman | old man | bull | duck flying | sun day | sky, above | rn name or young one | rnn praise jubilation | rnn nurse | Rnnwtt, the cobra goddess of the harvest |

Here are more ideograms and determinatives that you may find in your travels. Identify each in the space below.

Later, the addition of phonograms was a major development allowing the system to designate things and to express ideas.

Phonograms or Sound Signs

Monoliteral or **alphabetic** signs represent a single consonantal sound. Hieroglyphic writing avoided using vowels. The original pronunciation is unknown so any vocalization of the vowels is artificial. Pronunciation is noted below.

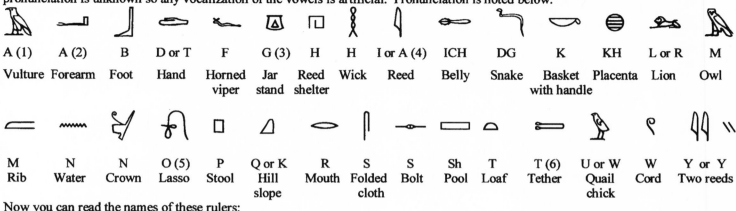

A (1)	A (2)	B	D or T	F	G (3)	H	H	I or A (4)	ICH	DG	K	KH	L or R	M
Vulture	Forearm	Foot	Hand	Horned viper	Jar stand	Reed shelter	Wick	Reed	Belly	Snake	Basket with handle	Placenta	Lion	Owl

M	N	N	O (5)	P	Q or K	R	S	S	Sh	T	T (6)	U or W	W	Y or Y
Rib	Water	Crown	Lasso	Stool	Hill slope	Mouth	Folded cloth	Bolt	Pool	Loaf	Tether	Quail chick	Cord	Two reeds

Now you can read the names of these rulers:

Write the name of the ruler in the space below the cartouche.
Find the first name in the Egyptian Museum in Cairo, and the others in the temples of the Greek period.
Notes: Pronounced as in (1) father, (2) day, (3) a hard g, (4) I or A as father if first sign, (5) as ua, o, w, u, (6) as tgh or th.

Phonograms or Sound Signs, Continued

There may be thousands of signs in ancient Egyptian writing, but only about 700 were frequently used. In addition to the monoliteral signs we call the alphabet, there are the **Biliteral** signs. They represent the sound of two consonants, and **Triliteral** signs representing the sound of three. Here are a few of the signs most frequently encountered. Some signs also represent abbreviations. These appear mostly on stone monuments or may be used to conserve space where a fuller writing may be less practical. The English translation of these signs is shown in Italics.

Biliteral signs

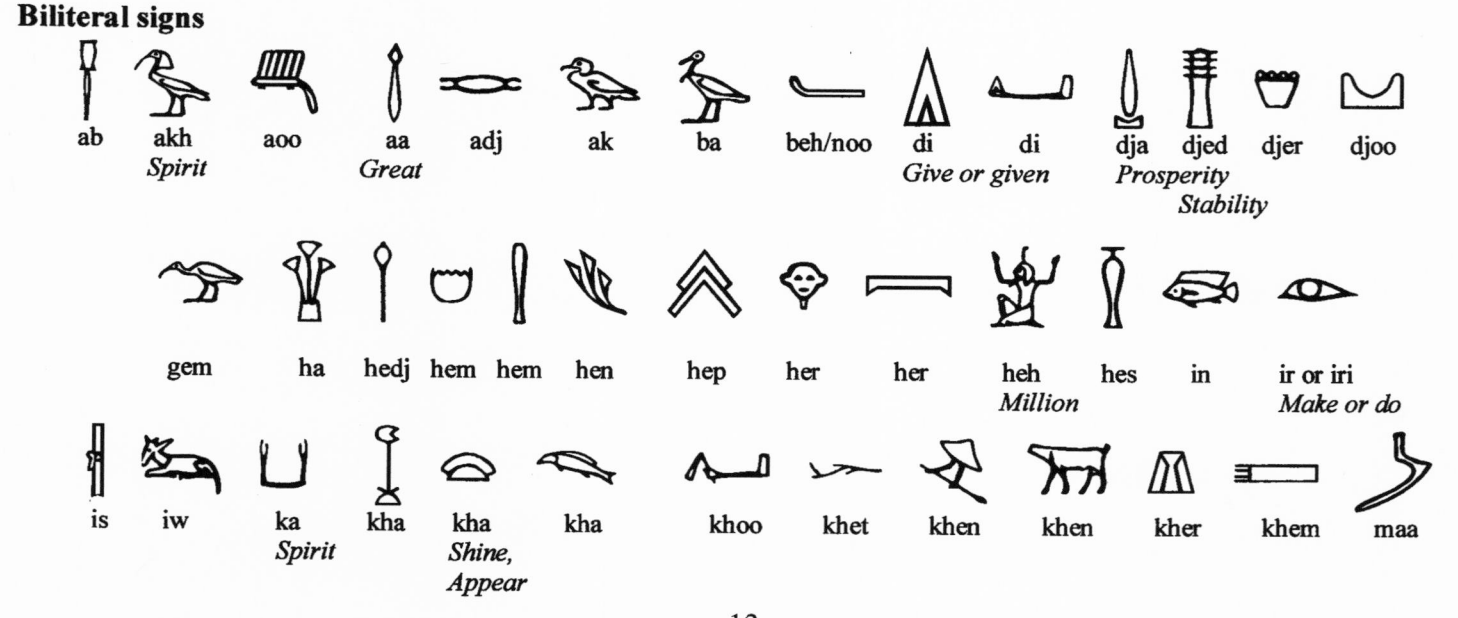

ab   akh   aoo   aa   adj   ak   ba   beh/noo   di   di   dja   djed   djer   djoo

akh — *Spirit*

aa — *Great*

di — *Give or given*

dja — *Prosperity*   djed — *Stability*

gem   ha   hedj   hem   hem   hen   hep   her   her   heh   hes   in   ir or iri

heh — *Million*

ir or iri — *Make or do*

is   iw   ka   kha   kha   kha   khoo   khet   khen   khen   kher   khem   maa

ka — *Spirit*

kha — *Shine, Appear*

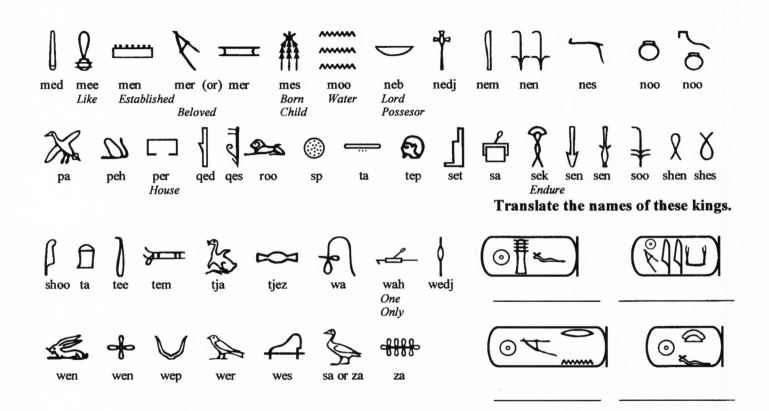

med	mee	men	mer (or) mer	mes	moo	neb	nedj	nem	nen	nes	noo	noo
	Like	*Established*	*Beloved*	*Born* *Child*	*Water*	*Lord* *Possesor*						

pa	peh	per	qed	qes	roo	sp	ta	tep	set	sa	sek	sen	sen	soo	shen	shes
		House									*Endure*					

Translate the names of these kings.

shoo	ta	tee	tem	tja	tjez	wa	wah	wedj
							One *Only*	

wen	wen	wep	wer	wes	sa or za	za

14

Here are some Triliteral signs

aha	ankh	asha	baz	dba	hat	heka	hetep	iwn	khenet	khenet	kheper	chenem
	Life				*Foremost*	*Ruler*	*Peace*				*Become*	*Associate*

kheroo	maa	medoo	menekh	moot	nedjem	nefer	nset	pkhr	renep	neter	roodj	sah
						Good *Beautiful*				*God*		

seba	setep	teeoo	tepy	usr	wadj	was	wehem	zia	zechem	zema	zenedj
	Chosen			*Power*	*Success*		*Repeat*				

Hieroglyphs do not always mean the same as the item pictured. For example, the owl sign usually means the letter *m*. The glyph for mouth (⟨⟩) means *r*. To indicate that the glyph actually means the item pictured a determinative stroke was used. The letter *r* (the mouth) with a short stroke (⟨⟩) means mouth or speech and not the letter *r*. Along with carrying sound value, these signs also carry word value and fall into the area of ideographic writing. The word *iri* (⟨⟩) "to make" or "to do", for example, can simply mean "eye" (⟨⟩) indicated by the single stroke (|), with feminine words showing the ending "t" (⟨⟩) in many, but not all cases.

Read the name of this god.

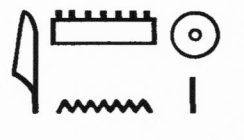

15

Now combine all three: Monoliteral, Biliteral, and Triliteral signs and name these kings.

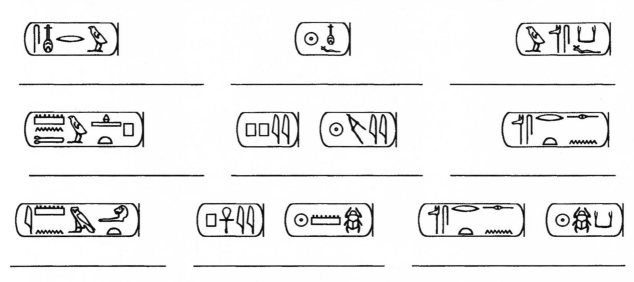

_____   _____   _____

_____   _____   _____

_____   _____   _____

NOTES:

Sign Groups and Abbreviations

Sign Groups make understanding hieroglyphic writing easier.

Royal Epithets

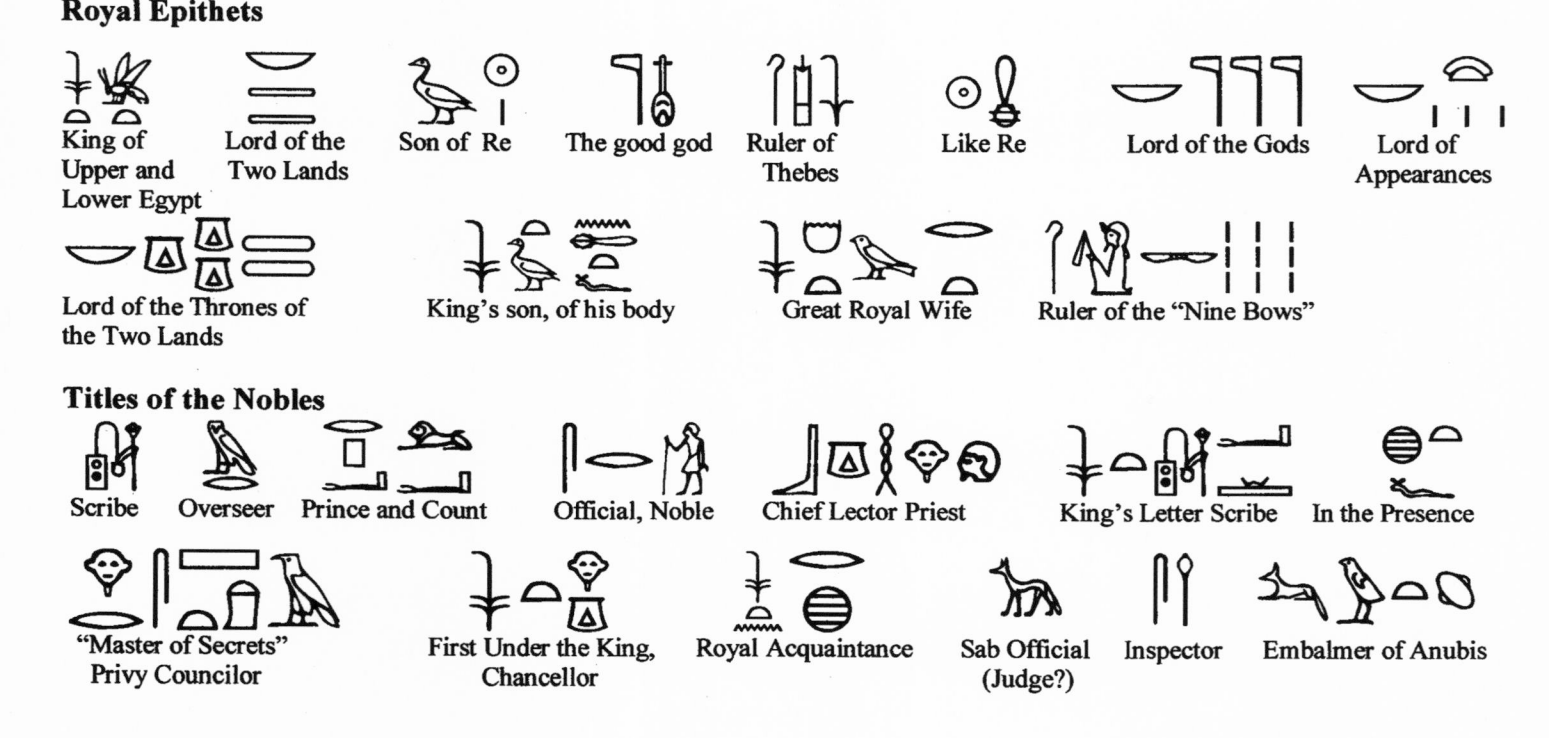

King of Upper and Lower Egypt | Lord of the Two Lands | Son of Re | The good god | Ruler of Thebes | Like Re | Lord of the Gods | Lord of Appearances

Lord of the Thrones of the Two Lands | King's son, of his body | Great Royal Wife | Ruler of the "Nine Bows"

Titles of the Nobles

Scribe | Overseer | Prince and Count | Official, Noble | Chief Lector Priest | King's Letter Scribe | In the Presence

"Master of Secrets" Privy Councilor | First Under the King, Chancellor | Royal Acquaintance | Sab Official (Judge?) | Inspector | Embalmer of Anubis

The Gods and Goddesses

Amen-Re

Wennefer, King of the Living
(Title of Osiris)

Osiris, Foremost of the West

Live, the Horus

Wosret, Goddess

Places

Horizon

Treasury

The Black Land,
Egypt

The Red Land,
Desert

The West

Most Select of Places
the Temples of Karnak at Thebes

The Necropolis

Other Words and abbreviations

Beloved

Forever

Eternity

The two ladies
Nebti Name

Life, prosperity
health

Life, stability,
dominion

All protection: life, stability,
dominion, health

Bread

Beer

Clothing

Beautiful/good

Evil/
evilly

Punish/
Punishment

Monument

May she/
you live

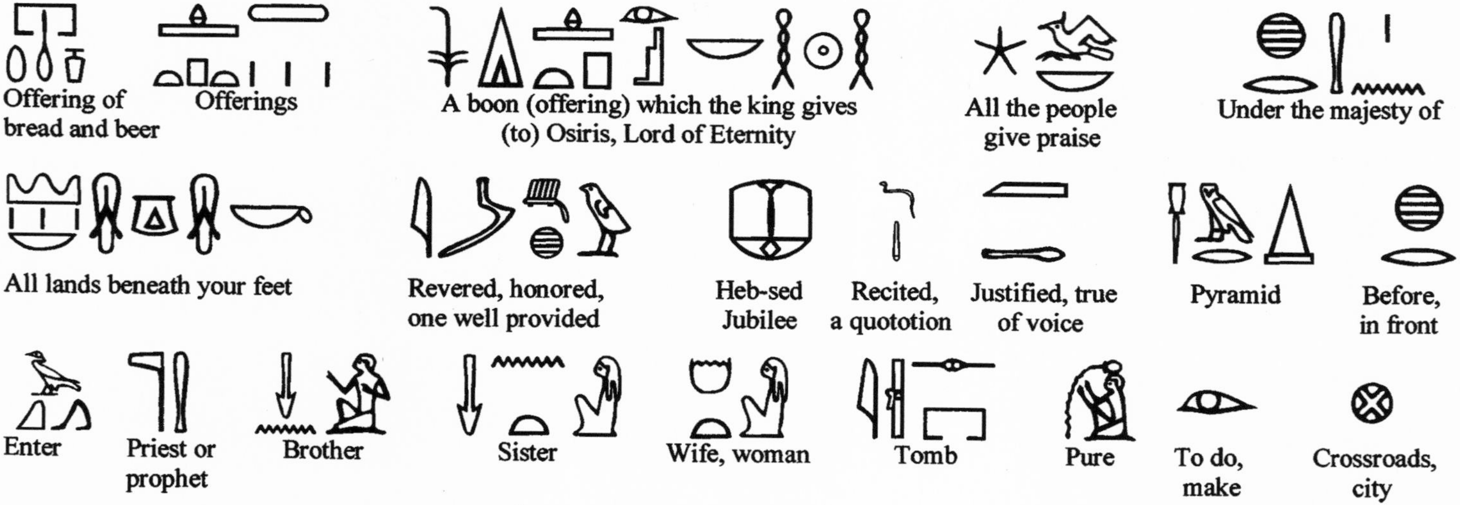

Offering of bread and beer	Offerings	A boon (offering) which the king gives (to) Osiris, Lord of Eternity	All the people give praise	Under the majesty of

All lands beneath your feet	Revered, honored, one well provided	Heb-sed Jubilee	Recited, a quototion	Justified, true of voice	Pyramid	Before, in front

Enter	Priest or prophet	Brother	Sister	Wife, woman	Tomb	Pure	To do, make	Crossroads, city

This king's mummy still rests in his golden coffin in the Valley of the Kings.

_____   _____   _____   _____

A Little Bit of Grammar

Suffix Pronouns: Singular   Suffix Pronouns: Plural

 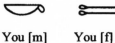 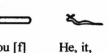 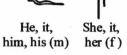 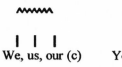 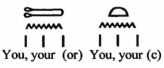

I, me, my	You [m]	You [f]	He, it, him, his (m)	She, it, her (f)	We, us, our (c)	You, your (or)	You, your (c)	They, them, their (c)

Conjunctions and prepositions

   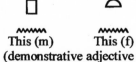 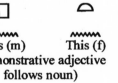 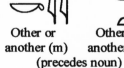

In, with, from	To, for (of direction to persons)	To, for (of direction to things)	This (m) (demonstrative adjective follows noun)	This (f)	And, together with	Other or another (m)	Other or another (f) (precedes noun)	Upon, concerning, because of

Everyone, anyone, every body	Not	Is, are	If, or as for

(m) masculine, (f) feminine, (c) common

Examples

There are two main types of sentences in Middle Egyptian. The first are verbal: those that contain a simple form of a finite verb. Second are the non-verbal: all those with no proper verb at all. Word order in the verbal sentence is usually: 1. Verb, 2. Subject, 3. Object, 4. Adverb or adverbial phrase (a preposition plus a noun).

1. A simple verbal sentence.

The priest enters the tomb. Lit. Enters (the) priest tomb this.

The subject, at times a noun as shown here and at other times a suffix as above, can be directly attached to a verb. This construction is called a *sḏm-f* form and functions for present and future tense, or *sḏm-n-f* form indicating simple past tense. (Pronounced sedjemef or sedjemenef) The verb sḏm    means "to hear," and is a paradigm used by Gardiner.

2   A simple sentence using *sḏm-n-f* past tense.

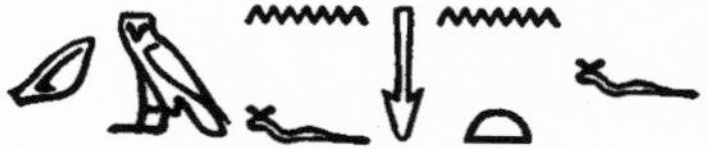

He heard his sister. Lit. Heard he sister his

Sentences using the verb "*iw*"    may act as either a main clause or a subordinate clause. This verb may at times have a suffix attached as the sentence subject.

3   A simple sentence using the verb "*Iw*" as copula (is, are, was).

He is in his house. Lit. Is he in his house.

Non-verbal sentence are those which have no actual verb in the predicate, or have one which expresses the force of a copula (is, are, was, etc.) The usual classifications are 1. Adverbial, 2. Nominal, 3. Adjectival. Following are examples of these:

4. Adverbial

The scribe (is) in the treasury. *Noun - Adverb or Preposition - Noun.*

5. Nominal

The scribe (is) his overseer. *Noun - Noun*

6. Adjectival

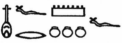

His monument (is) beautiful. *Adjective - Noun.* The adjective precedes the subject.
Lit. Beautiful (is) monument his.

7. Another example

Not   to do   I   evil   to   tomb   this

I did not do evil in respect of (to) this tomb

These are simple illustrations that hopefully will express the point. The reader is encouraged to consult grammatical texts for elaboration.

The Names of the Gods and Goddesses

A copy of the Book of the Dead was considered essential for a good and proper burial. This one, on the right, in the Cairo Museum shows the female papyrus owner in adoration and greeting before the god Osiris, and the "Four sons of Horus" protected by an encircling serpent to the left.

Among the best known Egyptian deities are those who attained national importance due to their cosmogonic or "creation myth" association. Some represent cosmic manifestations; Re, Nut, Geb, and Hapi for the sun, sky, earth, and the Nile, while others are more conceptual in nature such as Ma'at; truth and correct order. Some are chthonic (i.e. underworld) in focus such as Osiris, Anubis, and the Four Sons of Horus. Several important deities are shown here, but there are many more.

| Re | Amon-Re | A-N-P | P-T-H | AS-T |
| | | Anpu (Anubis) | Ptah | Isis |

Sobek *the crocodile deity was worshipped by Middle Kingdom rulers. As a national god, he became identified with Re as Sobek-Re and with the hawk Horus*

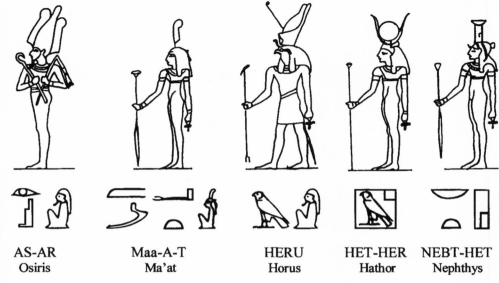

AS-AR	Maa-A-T	HERU	HET-HER	NEBT-HET
Osiris	Ma'at	Horus	Hathor	Nephthys

As you visit the monuments of Egypt, try to identify these and other deities. Draw their hieroglyphs and name them here.

Now check your new skill.

Read this inscription from
Tutankhamon's Alabaster cup.

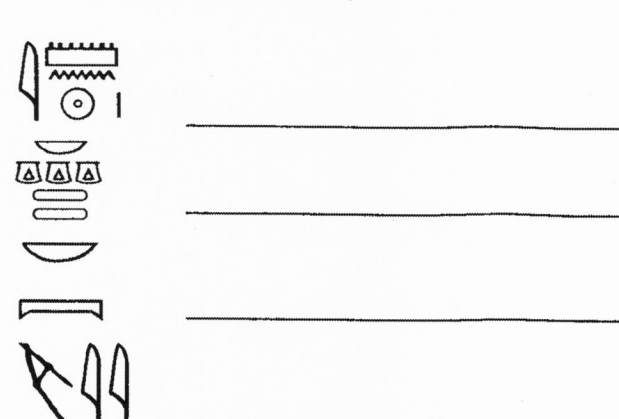

_____

_____

_____

You will find these glyphs on Merenptah's column
base in the Sculpture Garden at Memphis.

_____

_____

Read this inscription from Medinet Habu. He was the last great king on the throne of Egypt: Ramesses III

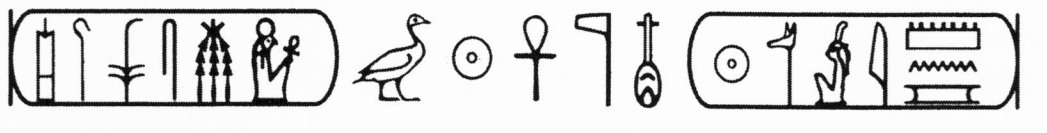

Ready? Let's kick the sand, climb the rocks, and
travel the corridors and causeways of the god kings.

The Great Pyramids, Tombs, and Sphinx of the Giza Plateau

Standing atop the limestone formation that makes up the Giza plateau, are in all probability, the most mysterious and compelling structures ever to be built by man; the **Pyramids of Giza**. These, along with the plateau's guardian, the Great Sphinx, have been the subject of more controversy in years past than anything else that one can conjure in the mind. And still today, when so much is known about these structures, the questions and debate still persist. What is known is that these are the last remaining wonders of the ancient world. These structures were not built by teaming masses of slaves, whipped almost to death by the overseers of a cruel Pharaoh as the historian Herodotus tells it, but rather by the populace of

Egypt during the time of the Nile flood in a sort of service to the living god of Egypt, the king. Many self-appointed "experts" have come forward with explanations as to the construction, alignment, and meaning of these structures, but few give credit to the genius of the ancient Egyptians as the foremost of master builders of their age. Perhaps, in our age of technology, it is inconceivable to us that a people could, with only very rudimentary tools, construct on a scale that would be daunting to most architects of our day. The simple fact is that they did, indeed, do it and have left behind for us to see the record of their means, if we only care to look with an unclouded eye.

It has recently been shown by archaeologists such as Mark Lehner and others, that much of the material used in the building of the pyramids was quarried locally at the Giza site and that a system of ramps was employed to move the massive blocks as the structure rose from the desert plateau.

In the past few years, the remains of the village, where the workmen who constructed the pyramids lived, has been unearthed by archaeologists. It shows us not a fantastic story of mythological beings from who knows where, but Egyptians who worked at the site daily and ate, slept, and had medical care provided for them by a large and well organized state.

The standard features of the developing pyramid complex by Sneferu, were continued on in the pyramids of

Giza. The mortuary temple and the valley temple were expanded and given a more formal character. The causeways at Giza stretch almost a kilometer and the valley temples are situated in the floodplain. The possibility exists that a harbor existed at the foot of the valley temples where the initial preparations (mummification) were made for burial upon the death of the king. Another aspect of this more formalized plan was the establishment of distinct cemeteries around the pyramid itself, with laid out streets and a sort of hierarchical arrangement of mastaba tombs as these structures are referred to. Here the nobility could be close to their king in death as they were in life. It should be pointed out however, that, with the exception of the First Dynasty, the king was not buried with a host of servants as it has at times been suggested. This rather distasteful practice ended with the demise of that First Dynasty.

Rather, it was their choice to be buried in the shadow of the pyramids, symbols of the sun god, perhaps representing the "ben-ben" which was the Egyptian word for the capstone of a pyramid or the tip of an obelisk, and may have represented the rays of the sun. The home of the original ben-ben was the ancient cult center of the sun god located at Heliopolis just to the northeast of Giza and, perhaps not coincidentally, on a line drawn through the southeast corners of the three main pyramids. The cardinal direction in ancient Egypt was not north, as in our culture, but rather south towards the headwaters of the Nile.

The **Great Pyramid** itself, was built by the pharaoh Khufu, (Khnum-khuf; "the god Khnum is his protection," or Khufu for short!), who came to power around 2550 BCE. The structure was called Akhet Khufu or "The Horizon of Khufu" and measures 755 feet at its base. It rises to a height of 482 feet minus the capstone which was removed some time in the past.

Amazingly, its orientation is only 3 degrees off true north and it was originally encased in fine white Turah limestone that must have made it a dazzling sight in the sun of Egypt!

Traditionally, the entrance was on the north side and aligned with the circumpolar stars that were the "immortal ones" because they never set when viewed from Egypt. The pyramid may be somewhat of a disappointment in the fact that there is really nothing to be seen apart from the structure itself. Once inside the most striking feature is the corbelled 28 foot high Grand Gallery that leads one up to the burial chamber. The chamber is 20 feet high by 34 feet long by 17 feet wide. It is entirely encased in granite with the king's sarcophagus, also of granite and sans lid, still in the chamber.

There is little doubt that this was indeed the final resting place of Khufu, although there are absolutely no inscriptions to tell one that. All the usually expected elements of the pyramid complex were present at one time but have mostly disappeared now. On the east side of the pyramid some black basalt pavement is all that can now be seen of the mortuary temple which was much larger than the preceding ones at Meidum and Dahshur.

Adjacent to this are boat pits which contained the so-called "Solar Barques" (boats) which may represent the Night and Day Barques of the Sun, and to date at least five more boat pits have been found in various locations around the pyramid. The pyramids of the three queens and the newly discovered satellite pyramid complete the main complex. The best guess is that the owners of these pyramids, moving north to south, are Queens Hetepheres, Meritetes and Henutsen with the satellite pyramid perhaps used in a cermonial way at the dedication of the main pyramid.

The **second of the three pyramids** on the plateau belongs to Khufu's son, **Khafre,** and is slightly smaller than that of his father. That it seems about the same size is due to the fact that it is built on a slightly higher elevation (10 m.) of the plateau than his fathers. Its slope is a bit sharper, about 53 degrees to Khufu's 51, and the lowest course of casing was in granite with the upper levels being of limestone. The pyramid was called "Great is Khafre". One of the most interesting aspects of this pyramid is the remains of the outer casing still visible towards the top. This gives us some clue of how this was completed and what the final "look" of the structure must have been. Close inspection of these casing stones reveals that they were not flush, but were backset by a few millimeters.

The question, then, is: was this a deliberate construction feature indicating perhaps that the blocks were cut before they were in place, or was this due to settling caused by the removal of the lower courses of casing. It is quite apparent that questions still remain to be answered!

The interior is not as complex as that of Khufu's pyramid. It has two descending passages, and upper and lower on the north side, a subsidiary chamber and a burial chamber. Both chambers are on an east-west axis with the black-granite sarcophagus on a north-south axis and very close to the vertical axis of the structure (i.e. almost, but not quite, on the N-S and vertical axis). A pit in the floor of the burial chamber may have held a canopic chest and would be the first in a pyramid. The entire pyramid complex is observable here with the mortuary temple built against the enclosure wall. In the Fifth Dynasty the mortuary temple would be built directly against the pyramid. The valley temple is quite well preserved and is built of gigantic core stones and encased with red granite. Additionally a satellite pyramid is in association with the pyramid and may have been used to hold the statues dedicated to the royal ka, or spiritual force of the king. The complex of the Great Sphinx of Khafre is discussed on a following page.

The **third pyramid** on the plateau is that of **Menkaure** who succeeded his father. His is the smallest of the three pyramids. Its most distinguishing feature is the 16 lower outer casing courses that are of red granite left undressed while the top is finished in the more usual Turah limestone. The pyramid was called "Menkaure is Divine" and it held very well preserved underground chambers. Although this structure is small by comparison to the two adjacent pyramids, the fact that it is made in great part of granite and not limestone, argues for longer and more costly construction time, as granite is much more difficult to quarry and transport.

The interior of the pyramid shows a carved panel motif and stylized false door decoration. Not since Djoser's Step Pyramid had the interior of a pyramid been decorated in any way. The descending passage leads to a decorated chamber, three portcullis blocks, and an antechamber which in turn leads to a passage to the burial chamber.

Additionally, off this final passage to the right is another chamber that contains six deep niches whose purpose is somewhat obscure. The burial chamber is carved out of bedrock and is encased in granite. The complex contains a mortuary temple, causeway, and valley temple where the famous triad statues, constructed of schist, and depicting Menkaura, Hathor, and a nome (district) deity were found. These are now in the Cairo Museum and are among the finest works of Egyptian art.

The queens' pyramids are unique in their own right. Two of them are of the "step pyramid" style, while the easternmost is of true pyramid form. Was this merely a result of their being incomplete, without final casing, or were they designed this way; the question remains open. In any case, the eastern pyramid was finished in granite and limestone casing. The T-shaped substructure of this pyramid may indicate that it was initially to be a satellite pyramid as seen in other complexes. Later it was likely used as a burial location for one of the queens of Menkaure and it was found to contain a granite sarcophagus. The pyramids all had mudbrick chapels in association with them which would seem to indicate that all were used for interment but only the middle one was found to contain a young female burial.

The Menkaure monument marks the end of pyramid building on the Giza plateau. The last major royal structure at Giza was that of Queen Khentkawes whose name means "formost-of-her-kas" in reference to her royal ancestors. Her mastaba lies south and west of the Great Sphinx approximately between the pyramids of Khafre and Menkaure.

Tombs on the Giza plateau

Giza Tombs: The Queens

When looking at the large cemeteries that sit to the east and west of the Great Pyramid of Khufu it is difficult to choose which of the many tombs to highlight. The task is made somewhat less difficult in that only selected ones are available for viewing.

In the eastern cemetery is the mastaba of **Queen Meresankh III**. It is numbered as mastaba G7530-40 on maps of the cemetery. The tomb chapel is not regularly visited, yet it is one of the best preserved in the cemetery. Her father was prince Kawab, a son of Khufu, and her mother was Hetepheres II, a daughter of Khufu and later queen to Khafre. The bones found in a lovely black granite sarcophagus in the floor of the western room of this mastaba appear to belong to queen Meresankh. This sarcophagus itself was apparently for Hetepheres, who had it re-inscribed for her daughter as a gift, indicating that the old queen outlived her daughter.

There are additional indications that the tomb was made for Hetepheres originally, but then made over for Meresankh. Hetepheres II likely lived into the reign of Shepseskaf at the end of Dynasty Four. The tomb is made up of three rooms; a main chamber, a west chamber and a north chamber. The main chamber is large for the period and shows scenes of both women, Hetepheres II and Meresankh, in various activities including the tomb owner, or perhaps we should say owners, viewing the produce from the estates and farming activities. Additionally boating and banqueting scenes are present.

The north wall of the main chamber has preserved the color of the hieroglyphic texts and the figures to an amazing degree. The west chamber contains a false door set centrally into an arrangement of palace facade doors on either side. Of interest here is a scene on the pillar between the doorways into the main room, which shows Meresankh standing before a smaller figure of a man. She holds the lotus flower in her left hand to her nose, with the stem looped to form a circle. The iconography here is representational of eternity. The lotus is representative of new life, as is seen in the famous figure from king Tutankhamon's tomb, where his head is seen rising out of a lotus blossom. The loop of the stem forms a "shen" or the solar symbol of eternity, as reflected in the cartouche surrounding the king's name.

Over the head of the queen is the inscription in five vertical lines reading right to left: *(1) "Beholder of Horus and Seth, great favorite, (2) king's daughter, of his body, (3) companion of Horus, (4) king's wife, beloved of him, (5) Meresankh."*

The north chamber is unique for the line of ten female statues. Above runs a long inscription: *"King's wife Hetepheres. Her daughter, beholder of Horus and Seth, great favorite, companion of Horus, consort of he who is beloved of the Two Ladies, follower of Horus, King's daughter of his body, beloved companion of Horus, royal wife, Meresankh."* The statues are perhaps female members of the royal family.

False Doors and Slab Stela

The false door of Mereruka at Saqqara, VI th. Dynasty

Beginning in the Fourth Dynasty at the time of Khufu, certain highly placed officials began to build what are known as mastaba tombs to the west and later to the east of the Great Pyramid of the king. A location in the shadow of the pyramid undoubtedly needed the permission of the king and many of the inscriptions left to us indicate that such was the case.

These tombs, simple in plan, contained two niches in the eastern face of the structure. The southernmost of these niches was the largest and was the place of offerings to the deceased. In this recess the so-called slab-stela was placed. Usually, these depicted the deceased seated before a table of offerings piled with bread loaves, with other types of offerings identified beside it. The slab-stela would also contain the name of the deceased and their titles along with, perhaps, a short prayer in the form of the *"hotep-di-nisw"* (a-boon-which-the-king-gives) formula.

Later, as small chapels developed in these mastaba tombs, probably due to the wish for a more elaborate place for offerings and a greater "show", the slab stela developed into a component of the new and larger *false door*. The slab stela became the rectangular tablet set above the central niche of the false door and the door itself became what archaeologists refer to as the focal point of the tomb. This was the spot where any activity regarding the cult of the deceased's spirit, the "ka", was undertaken. The ka lived in the tomb and it was necessary to furnish offerings for it's continued welfare, necessitating the need of a place where this could occur. The door functioned as a place where the ka could pass from the burial chambers, usually hidden below ground, to the more public rooms of the tomb chapel.

The door itself usually consisted of several slabs of stone, arranged symmetrically in a niched order, upon which offering formulae and certain

31

prayers and wishes for the well being of the deceased were inscribed. Initially, the doors were pieced together from several pieces of stone, but later were carved from a solid slab to reflect this style. On occasion they were painted a red color to imitate the more costly red granite, as these doors were usually made from limestone.

In front of the door was placed an additional, horizontal slab (or low table) to receive the offerings to the spirit.

Beginning in the Sixth Dynasty, some include a statue in the form of the deceased emerging through the door to receive the offerings. The tombs of Idu and Mereruka show excellent examples of this concept.

Following are some early examples of design and reading of these false doors intended to help you become acquainted with their texts. Sharpen your glyphic skills.

The Tombs of Two Officials

The mastabas of **Idu** and **Qar** are located in the eastern cemetery to the south of the pyramid causeway and near the large mastaba of Kawab, a son of Khufu.

When visiting these tombs it will be necessary to locate an attendant to open them, but these people are in fact, never far off and await the opportunity to serve you. Be advised however, that baksheesh (a tip or gratuity) will be expected for this service.

These two tombs are located side by side and are numbered G 7101 (Qar) and G 7102 (Idu) respectively. Each has something to recommend it to the traveler and student of the ancient Egyptian language.

The superstructure of these tombs has almost entirely disappeared. The chapel of Qar, whose "good name" was **Meryre-nefer**, can be dated to the reign of the pharaoh Pepy I or later (6th Dynasty) based upon titles found in association to the deceased. It is probable that Idu, whose tomb is adjacent, was the father of Qar based upon philological grounds referencing the titles of the two.

Of great interest in Qar's tomb are the scenes of an Old Kingdom funerary procession, one of the earliest known examples. Descending two sets of stairs and making a right turn at the entrance to the court, one enters the tomb. Here, on the north wall of the court, the funerary procession can be seen. Looking directly ahead, several statues are seen in the adjacent room. Above these runs a line of glyphs reading from right to left: *"Tenant farmer (gardener?) of the pyramid Mennefer-Meryre, royal letter scribe in the presence, Sab-official (judge), overseer of the scribes of all the works, Qar."* Entering the small room to the right of the statues, the false door of Qar is seen on the west wall telling us (outer left vertical column) that he is *"Well provided before Osiris Sab-official, overseer of scribes, master of secrets (privy-counselor or secretary?) of every command, Qar"*.

A Boon which the King Gives: The formula over the entrance to the tomb of Idu.

This is a complete rendering of the Htp-di-nisu formula of the nobleman Idu as found over the entrance to his tomb (G-7102) in cemetery 7000 at the Giza plateau.

The text runs left to right starting the third line from the top of the architrave which is composed of six blocks set on natural rock above the entrance to the tomb. They are the only existing masonry blocks used in the chapel, which is cut from natural rock. Idu is shown wearing a short pointed skirt, a broad collar, wristbands and a wig. He is holding a staff diagonally in his right hand and a *sekhem* or scepter of authority in his left.

(1) *A boon-which-the-king-gives and a boon-which-Anubis-gives, foremost of the divine booth, he who is upon his hill, who is in Ut (place of embalming), lord of the sacred land, lord of a good burial in the necropolis, and a boon-which-Osiris-gives: that he be well buried in his tomb which is in the West, that he travel upon the goodly ways, (2) that he be accompanied by his kas, that his hand be taken by the great god, that he be led upon the splendid roads upon which the well-provided travel, that he be lifted up to the great god as a well-provided one, (3) whom the great god loves; lord of*

reverence, possessor of a good burial in the necropolis. May invocation offerings of bread, beer and cakes go forth for him in the West very greatly. May he be glorified very greatly by the lector (priests) and embalmers, (4) at the New Year's festival, at the Thoth festival, at the first of the year, at the Wag-feast, at the Feast of Sokar, at the great festival, at the fire-lighting festival, at the Sadj festival, at the going forth of Min, (5) at the half-month and month festival, at the seasons festival, at the beginning of all decades, at all great festivals, and throughout the course of every day: a thousand of oryx, a thousand bulls, a thousand ro geese, a thousand trp geese, (6) a thousand set birds, a thousand se birds, a thousand pidgeons, a thousand of clothing, a thousand of linen, a thousand of bread, a thousand cakes, a thousand of beer, as pure bread of the great god, for the overseer of the distribution of divine offerings in the two houses, one well provided before the great god, (7) the one before the king's head, staff of the rekhyt (people), pillar of Kenmet, master of secrets of judgement, priest of Maat, royal letter scribe in the presence, overseer of scribes of the meret serfs, well provided before Anubis who is on his hill, who is in Ut (place or city of embalming), (8: vertical before the figure of Idu) royal letter scribe in the presence, overseer of scribes of the meret serfs, Idu.

Entering the Tomb of Idu: The curse

Upon entering the tomb of Idu, make note of the inscription on the right hand side of the west doorjamb, in one vertical line, reading from top to bottom. This is one of a very few "curses" that appear in tombs. Some of these give warning that the transgressor will be seized around the neck by the akh (spirit) and have it wrung like a bird. The usual adjuration however, is that the person entering the tomb not be "unclean" or "impure"; this is the main force of the curse at Idu's doorway. The Egyptians did employ curses in various ways, mainly as execration texts aimed at an enemy of some sort, in love magic directed towards jealous or nefarious ends (see Numbers 5:11-31 for a Biblical example of this type). Letters to the dead are also found where a deceased relative is called upon for help in attaining some desired end.

Translate the curse, and then enter the tomb...if you dare.

As for _____ _____ who shall enter _____ _____ not

purifying himself as the purification of a god, one shall make a _____

for him because of it _____.

The 'Ka" of Idu is represented in graphic fashion as he rises up his burial shaft from the tomb chamber below with arms outstretched to receive the funerary offerings

Translation of the false door above the statue of Idu.

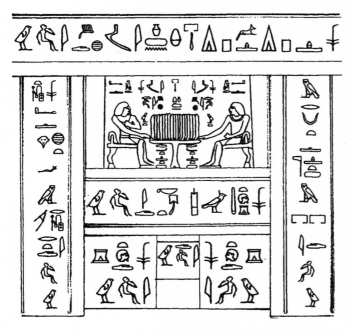

Drawing of the false door in the tomb of Idu at Giza.

Top line: *A boon which the king gives, and which Anubis gives, that invocation offerings of bread, beer, cakes, go forth for the well provided Idu.*

Slab stela (center), above table of bread: Center-
An invocation offering of bread, beer and cakes for
At the top on each side- *The well provided king's letter scribe, Idu.*

Vertical at right: *Overseer of the distribution of divine offerings in the two houses, Idu.*

Vertical at left: *King's letter scribe in the presence, overseer of the scribes of the "meret" serfs, Idu.*

Below slab stela: *He who is at the head of the king (chamberlain?), staff of the "rekhyet" people, pillar of Kenmet, Idu.*

Bottom center section: Left - *He who is at the head of the king, Idu.*

Bottom center section: Right - *He who is at the head of the king, Idu.*

Center, drum cylinder: *Idu.*

The Royal Boats of Khufu

Lying in close proximity to the Great Pyramid of King Khufu are pits for a number of boats. To date seven pits have been discovered; five lying to the east and two to the south. The two pits on the southern side were discovered in 1954 while clearing an area that had not previously been excavated. Upon clearing the sand, limestone slabs with plastered mud were discovered. All had been sealed with plaster in ancient times and bore the royal seal of Radjedef, the successor of Khufu, impressed into the plaster.

Of the seven pits discovered, only the two southern pits contained actual boats. They differ in form from the others in that they are long and narrow rather than boat shaped. The eastern boat pits proved to be empty, as perhaps the shape of a boat was deemed sufficient to represent the vessel itself. This is not unique in Egyptian archaeology as other empty boat pits in the shape of a vessel have been found at such places as Abydos in Middle Egypt dating from earlier dynasties.

The boat now on display in her own museum next to the pyramid, measures approximately 142 feet in length and 19ft. 6in. wide at the midpoint, with a calculated displacement of 45 tons. The magnificent craft would have floated about 15 inches clear of the water amidships. Equally amazing is the method employed in the boat's construction. Made of cedarwood, the separate parts had unique U-shaped holes, which enabled the boat to be literally "stitched" together. This was done with ropes of fibers or perhaps leather thongs with "batten" strips lashed beneath the ribs, each made to fit in one place only, to ensure a seal.

The second boat pit to the south was investigated in 1985 and found to contain the disassembled parts of what appears to be a similar boat. Apparently, these boats were intended to be disassembled and buried in this fashion. The obvious question, then, is: "why?" As the boat resembles the so-called "Solar Boat" or "wia" seen in illustrations in which the sun god traveled across the heavens, the implication here is that this vessel is of a symbolic nature. The wood however showed marks of the lashings having tightened in place, and thereby indicating that the vessel had, in fact, been used in the water at some point.

Here we must look to certain magical implications for our explanation. It is most likely significant that both of these boats lie outside of the "temenos" or enclosure wall that surrounds the pyramid and marks off the "holy" area. Any items that were connected with the funeral would have been seen as being imbued with certain power. The dismantling of these boats would have been an apotropaic measure, being buried nearby, but outside, the funerary area. Undoubtedly, these boats were in some way connected with the final journey of the pharaoh Khufu.

The Great Sphinx

In association with the pyramid of Khafre is the **Great Sphinx**. This is carved from the bedrock at the base of the causeway and close by the valley temple. In form it is a portrait of Khafre on the body of a lion and is both a symbol of royalty and a guardian. It also has very unique religious attributes that stem from New Kingdom times when it was seen as an image of the sun god. This association may have roots that are more ancient, but this is lost in the mists of time.

Directly in front of the animal lies the Sphinx temple, which is undoubtedly dedicated to it, but again, since there are no Old Kingdom texts that refer to either temple or beast, the association must be inferred archaeologically rather than textually. The same style of design layout visible in the adjacent valley temple of Khafre is visible here with recesses for 10 statues rather than the 12 of the Khafre temple.

The temple has two sanctuaries, one to the east and the other to the west, perhaps associated with the rising and setting sun. Mark Lehner has pointed out that, at the time of summer solstice, the sun, when viewed from the Sphinx temple, sets just between the pyramids of Khufu and Khafre. This is of course reflective of the hieroglyph for horizon, akhet, which represents the sun setting between two mountains. The cultic significance here cannot be ignored, nor can the association with the name of the Great Pyramid of Khufu, Akhet or horizon, the name also given to the entire necropolis here at Giza.

Dream Stela

This stela reveals how Prince Tuthmosis IV became king.

The Egyptians called the Great Sphinx Horemakhet or Horus in the Horizon and revered him as a god, a form of Horus. According to the tale, the god spoke to the young prince Tuthmosis IV as he lay sleeping in the shadow of the sphinx to escape the midday sun. The god promised to make the young prince king if he would clear away the sand from the sphinx. Because of many irregularities and errors in the text, the stela was considered by Adolph Erman and several others to be a late restoration of the original, produced between the Twenty-first and Twenty-second Dynasties and the Saitic times. Recent investigations however, have cleared up most of Ermans' objections to the stela being of Eighteenth Dynasty date, especially those regarding the damage done by the Atonists during the Amarna Period. The question of its literary style, as a folk-tale like narrative with few parallels to other royal records of the period, still remains. Without question, however, Tuthmosis IV expanded the solar significance of the cult of Horemakhet at Giza. He refers to the sphinx as Horemakhet-Khepri-Re-Atum and omits Amon-Re from the stela altogether. As such, this deity assumes a role as both sun god and as royal legitimizer in the north at Giza.

The stela is eleven feet and ten inches in height and seven feet two inches in width with fully the lower one third having flaked off; thus over half of the inscription is lost to us. It is made of red granite and stands between the paws of the great beast.

The lunette at the top of the stela shows an adoration scene of Tuthmosis IV offering to the god Horemakhet in sphinx form.

The following translation reproduces only the introduction and the vision due to space considerations. The vision however, may be regarded as the most significant section of the monument.

Introduction

(1) Year 1, third month of the first season (Inundation season; roughly mid-July to mid-November), day 19, under the majesty of Horus: Mighty Bull, Perfect in Risings; The Two Ladies: Enduring in Kingship like Atum; Horus of Gold: Mighty of Sword, Subduing the Nine Bows; King of Upper and Lower Egypt; Menkheperure, Son of Re: Tuthmosis kha khau; beloved of Horemakhet, given life, stability, dominion, like Re, forever.

(2) Live the Good God, son of Atum, Protector of Harakhte, living image of the All-Lord; sovereign, born of Re; excellent inheritor of Khepri; beautiful of face like the ruler, his father; who came forth well equipped with the form of Horus upon him; the king of Upper and Lower Egypt, beloved of the gods, who possess favor with the ennead of gods; who purifies Heliopolis,

(3) who satisfies Re; who beautifies Memphis; who presents Ma'at to Atum, who offers it to Him-who-is-South-of-His-Wall; who makes monuments of daily offering to Horus; who does all things, who seeks benefits for the gods of Upper and Lower Egypt; who builds their temples of white limestone; who endows all their offerings; son of Atum, of his body, Tuthmosis kha khau, like Re;

(4) heir of Horus upon his throne, Menkheprure, given life.

The Vision

(8) One of those days it came to pass that the king's son, Tuthmosis, came at the time of midday, and he rested in the shadow of this great god. Sleep and a dream seized him at the hour when the sun was at the highest,

(9) and he found the majesty of this revered god speaking with his own mouth, as a father speaks with his own son saying: "Behold you me! See me, my son Tuthmosis. I am thy father Horemakhet-Khepri-Re-Atum, who will give to thee the kingship

(10) upon earth at the head of the living. You shall wear the White Crown and the Red Crown upon the throne of Geb, the hereditary prince. The land shall be yours in its length and width, that which the eye of the All-Lord shines upon. The provisions of the Two Lands shall be yours, the great tribute of all the countries, the duration of a time great in years. My face is yours, my desire (heart) is toward you. You shall be to me a protector

(11) for my manner is as (though) I were ailing, all my limbs in ruin. The sand of this desert upon which I used to be has reached me; in order to cause you to turn to me to have that done which I have desired. I know that you are my son, my protector; approach, behold, I am with you, I am

(12) your leader."

When he had finished this speech, the king's son awoke hearing this -- -- ; he understood the words of this god and kept silent in his heart. He said: "Come, let us travel to our temple in the city; so that they may protect the offerings for this god

(13) which we bring for him: oxen -- and all types of vegetables; and we shall give praise to those who came before, -- -- the statue of Khafre, made for Atum-Re-Horemakhet-----

This translation follows and updates that offered by James Henry Breasted in his *Ancient Records of Egypt*, Chicago, 1906 which is itself a compilation of several sources.

The Necropolis of Saqqara

Along with Giza, Saqqara comprises the main necropolis (city of the dead) of the ancient capital of Memphis. It is the larger of the two and it's central feature is the great third dynasty step pyramid complex of king **Djoser** dating to c. 2650 BCE. It is the first pyramid of any type to be built in Egypt and the first structure made completely of stone. The structure takes the mastaba concept of the first and second dynasties a step further by superimposing several of these mastaba structures, one on top of the other, to create a six-step pyramid. This was done by **Imhotep** the royal architect and later demigod of the Greek Period. The religious and philological implications of the structure become obvious when one realizes that the shape is that of the glyphic symbol for stairway (⌐ △) and so perhaps this was Djoser's pathway to ascend to heaven.

A large enclosure wall of limestone bricks surrounded the structure itself. The wall has been reconstructed in the southeast corner of the complex. The only entrance to the complex was through a long colonnaded passage. The columns are of an engaged nature that shows a reluctance to incorporate freestanding columns at this very ancient date. They form alcoves, which held statuary, in all likelihood.

Other buildings devoted to the cult of the dead pharaoh, included the so-called *heb-sed* or jubilee court. Here, immortalized in stone, is a reconstruction of the temporary structure where the king celebrated his thirtieth year of reign.

This court also held structures that represented Upper and Lower Egypt, the House of the South and House of the North, which again were temporary structures now made permanent in stone and thus depicting a united Egypt. On the north side of the pyramid, the *serdab* or hiding place, can be found where a statue of Djoser (a copy, as the original is in the Cairo museum) looks toward the northern stars. The king hoped to join his ancestors in the heavens and so this orientation towards the imperishable stars (i.e. the stars that never set). Alongside this are the remains of the mortuary temple.

At the southern end of the complex is the so-called South Tomb, which is built into the enclosure wall. This may have a connection to the ancient burials of the royalty in Abydos. A large system of underground galleries which are unfortunately, not accessible to the public, lie beneath the pyramid. Examples of the decoration from these galleries can be viewed in the Cairo museum.

To the south of the complex stands the pyramid (or what is left of it!) of **Unas**, last king of the Fifth Dynasty. This is the first pyramid to contain the texts that are now known as the *Pyramid Texts*. Here the walls of the inner chambers are covered with the lengthy writings that are a collection of invocations and magic spells intended to help the king's soul overcome the difficulties and provide the basis for the Coffin

Texts of the Middle Kingdom and then finally the Book of the Dead in the New Kingdom.

There are several interesting mastaba tombs in the area. As at Giza, many are not open to the public, but some that are show wonderful examples of glyphs from the Old Kingdom times. One of particular interest, in the area of the pyramid of Teti, is the tomb belonging to **Mereruka**, who indicates that his *good name* was Meri, the Vizier, Overseer of the Town, and Inspector of the prophets of the Pyramid of Teti. He is joined by his wife, Wa'tet-Khet-Hor, and son Meryteti, (Dynasty VI). This tomb shows depictions of the tomb owner and his wife fishing and fowling in a canoe in the marshes, observing various industries, listening to music and making offerings. The focal point of the tomb however, is the statue of the deceased, Mereruka, striding forth from the false door to receive funerary offerings. It is one of the best of its kind to be seen.

Around the corner from Mereruka is the mastaba of **Kagemni**, whose *good name* was Memi, the Vizier, Inspector of the prophets, and Overseer of the town of the Pyramid of Teti. Of special interest here is a scene in the pillared hall on the east wall. The scene is of cattle fording water (the Nile?) and men in boats. The men in the boats appear to be making gestures of a magical nature in order to aid the cattle in their crossing and to repel crocodiles that lurk along the banks and in the marshes. Scenes of this type can be observed in several Old Kingdom mastaba tombs.

The heb-sed court at Djoser's Step Pyramid complex.

Within the walls of the Step Pyramid complex is located the so-called heb-sed or jubilee court. Here the king would perform the ceremonies associated with this festival, designed to bring renewed vitality to the pharaoh. This was traditionally done only once every thirty years but most kings celebrated it at least once during their reign. The structures are merely facades and there is speculation as to whether this court was, in fact, ever used or was constructed for, as many suspect, representational purposes only.

Dahshur and Meidum: The True Pyramids Appear

The pyramid concept, which was begun at Saqqara with the Step Pyramid, was continued at Meidum and Dahshur. Until recently it was commonly believed that the builder of the so-called "collapsed pyramid" at Meidum was the Pharaoh Huni at the end of the Third Dynasty. Indications are, however, that this pyramid was the initial attempt of the Pharaoh Sneferu at making a true pyramid from what had begun as a step pyramid. That this is so is based on the fact that the name of Huni never appears on any of the ancient records at the Meidum site and the name of Sneferu does. Additionally, and perhaps more compelling, is that the site in ancient times was, indeed, called Djed Sneferu or "Sneferu Endures".

The Meidum pyramid was built in stages like the pyramid of Djoser at Saqqara and consisted of eight "steps" or stages that were completed by the end of Sneferu's 14th year. At this time the court seems to have made a move to the north to the site of Dahshur, perhaps to be closer to the Delta region for administrative purposes. The site of Meidum was abandoned with the pyramid left in its initial step style and, according to at least one theory, not filled out to true pyramid form until the end of Sneferu's reign.

In the intervening years, two more large pyramids were built by this king, making him the undisputed master of raising these incredible stone edifices. Records additionally show that, in the last years of Sneferu's reign, his workers returned to this site and finished constructing the pyramid in smooth sides of Turah limestone.

The Meidum pyramid today consists of a three level core surrounded by a large mound of debris. There are several theories for the structure's strange appearance today, with the most credible being that it has simply been quarried away over the years. W.M.F. Petrie indicated as much when he recorded that this process was still going on during his sojourn in Egypt.

The more popular theory, of course, is that it collapsed while under construction due to a lack of an understanding of the principles necessary to build a smooth sided pyramid. That this is not so is indicated by the lack of any remains of Fourth Dynasty material found in recent excavations, including bodily remains, which one might expect to find under such catastrophic conditions.

The pyramid and its' complex shows several features which were to become standard in all pyramid construction. The entrance was found on the north side with a long descending passage that led to the burial chamber. This chamber differed from that of Djoser's in its construction. Whereas Djoser's burial chamber complex was below ground, here the architects were striving to create a room within the pyramid structure itself. They incorporated the technique of corbelling for the first time in the inner chamber, each block above a particular point projecting inward until a meeting of the walls was achieved. Additionally, traces of a rectangular enclosure wall survive, and to the south there may have been a small subsidiary pyramid.

On the eastern side a chapel was discovered, but it's two round-topped stelae were blank, and a causeway was found leading to the south-east which may indicate the presence of a valley temple although none has been found. A mastaba field was located to the north of the complex and it was here that the famous Meidum Geese and the sublime statues of **Rahotep** and his wife **Nofret** (all in the Cairo Museum) were found. All of these elements would be seen in later pyramids as components of the classic pyramid complex.

At the site of Dahshur, some 25 miles to the north, Sneferu constructed two more pyramids. Today these are known as the Bent Pyramid (to the south) and the Red or North Pyramid. It is with the building of this Red or North pyramid that the architects finally succeeded in building an elegantly designed and efficiently constructed true pyramid. Both of these structures show elements that would become standard in pyramid complex architecture, with the Bent Pyramid showing the first Valley Temple construction.

The unique shape of this pyramid has again caused some discussion. This structure may have started out much smaller but more steeply sloped and then had subsidence problems. The situation required the addition of a stabilizing wall around the structure that gave it less of a slope but may have actually increased the stresses on the pyramid. This,

then, in all likelihood, necessitated the severe change in slope (from an initial 60 degrees to 55 and finally a slope of 43 degrees at the bend), to prevent a feared structural failure. It was hoped that this "bend" would lighten the load on the vaults.

The North Pyramid lacks any significant remains of a causeway and very scant remains of a Valley Temple, although many feel that this is, indeed, the final resting-place of Sneferu. Here a long passage leads from the entrance, well up the north face of the structure, to two antechambers at ground level. A passage high up on the wall of the second antechamber, made accessible by a modern staircase, leads to the burial chamber. All of these rooms show the continued use of corbelling for the roof. The upward movement of the burial chamber within the pyramid may reflect a changing religious attitude in the king's relationship with the gods, as he becomes increasingly identified with the solar deity. The pyramid, of course, has direct cosmological connections with this solar cult, as it is soon after this that the king becomes identified as the son of Re.

The Standard of Dahshur/Meidum

43

Luxor Temple: *Ipet-Resyt*, The Southern Harem

The temple of Luxor, which was linked to Karnak in ancient times by a paved limestone street about a mile and one half in length with stone sphinxes on either side, is the second major temple structure on the east side of the Nile at Luxor. This street was built by Nectanebo I in the 30th Dynasty. The Egyptian name for the temple was *Ipet-Resyt* or the Southern Harem. It's purpose was as a southern palace for the god Amon to reside in with his consort Mut during the Opet festival which was held during the second month of the season of Nile flood. This once yearly journey of Amon and Mut would be carried out amidst a great celebration of people drinking, dancing and eating in the streets while the divine couple were transported in their barques from Karnak to this sanctuary. Here they would spend almost three weeks in honeymoon while their son Khonsu was conceived. The festival was considerably lengthened over time from the original eleven days

The great pylon that forms the front of the temple is guarded by two great seated statues of **Ramesses II** and two obelisks, of which only the eastern one remains. The pylon shows scenes of the Battle of Kadesh fought in Syria against the Hittites. The following open court of Ramesses II is noticeably out of line with the rest of the temple. This may have been done to facilitate the incorporation of the temple of **Tuthmosis III** that previously was outside the temple proper. The statues that stand between the columns in this court now depict Ramesses II but may have originally been placed by **Amenhotep III**. The small figure seen

Ramesses II at Luxor Temple.

walking behind his leg is queen Nefertari.

The journey of Amon, Mut and Khonsu is depicted on the west and east side walls of the great colonnade showing the outward trip and the return to Karnak respectively. Unfortunately, these walls have been reduced to less than one third of their original height. The colonnade itself was built by Amenhotep III and decorated by **Tutankhamon** to celebrate the revival of the god's cult following the Amarna period. This, along with his tomb in the Valley of the Kings, are Tutankhamon's sole surviving monuments.

The court of Amenhotep III is nearly complete and thought to be one of the finest of its kind to have survived from ancient Egypt. Beyond this lies the hypostyle hall of 32 columns which is not in the best of condition, although recent work has revived it somewhat.

Alexander the Great rebuilt the sanctuary and he is shown on the walls as pharaoh. This was as far as the barque of Amon traveled and here was set upon a pedestal. The ceremonies actually ended in the next room, the so-named 'birth room', with the annual union of the queen mother and the god. This was of course, symbolic in nature. The purpose was to renew the king and his ka, the direct expression of his royal and divine nature, and to confirm his power. The pharaoh thus re-engendered, emerged from the temple invigorated with new wisdom and power and as the protector of Maat, the correct order of the universe.

King's names you may find at Luxor Temple

Ramesses II (meryamon) Usermaatre Setepenre   1279-1212

Tuthmosis III Menkheperre   1504-1450

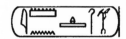

Amenhotep III (hekawaset) Nebmaatre   1386-1349

Tutankhamon (hekaiunushema) Nebkheperure   1334-1325

Alexander the Great Meryamun Setepenre 323-317

Draw the names and identify other rulers you may find.

45

Karnak Temples: *Ipet-Iset,* The Most Select of Places

To understand the nature of the Egyptian temple the underlying mythology must be considered. This structure and the surrounding area marked off by the outer (temenos) wall is representative of the sacred area which emerged from the watery abyss at the beginning of creation. These waters, called Nun, brought forth a mound of land and upon this all creation came into being. The varying Egyptian cosmogonies (creation myths) tell different stories of how this happened, but it is through this that Mankind was created and so this time was revered by the Egyptians as a manifestation of the power of divinity. All of Egypt's temples are, at least in theory, on an east-west axis to follow the path of the sun on it's daily journey across the heavens as was laid down at the time of this creation.

According to texts found at the temple of Horus at Edfu, the form of the first temple was set forth by the gods themselves; outer enclosure wall to separate the sacred area from the outside and inner structures to protect the exact site of creation and mark it as sacred. As one enters the temple area, a journey of both spatial and temporal nature begins to take place, for the deeper one moves in towards the innermost sanctuary containing the shrine or naos, the farther back in time one travels. This feeling of journeying in time and space in accentuated by the rising up of the floor and the lowering of the ceiling until one stands before the god at the beginning of time to experience the *sp-tpy* or the mythological First

Karnak Temples: a complex built on a scale of giant gods.

occasion. The temple of Karnak is no exception to this plan, but rather is on a scale not to be found in other Egyptian temples. A single visit to this site can only give a hint of the vastness of this *holy city*. What survives today is, in the main, from the New Kingdom times forward. There is, however a Middle Kingdom component to the site in the form of an area that today looks like a kind of court. Here, it is certain, stood a complex constructed in limestone by **Senworset I**. As with all temples, only the priests and those who were in service to the god were allowed to enter. Pharaoh also was welcome here as the beloved son of the god Amen and, in theory at least, the only true priest of the cult. These temples should not be seen in any way as an equivalent of a modern house of worship as the general public was not allowed to penetrate their mysteries. The approach to the first pylon, the largest in Egypt, is down an avenue of curly-horned sphinxes, the body of a lion and the head of a ram, which represent one of the forms of the god Amen-Re. Between the paws of this creature is a statue of his son **Ramesses II**. Five more pylons must be passed through before reaching the sanctuary at the heart of the mystery and, once here, the traveler finds that the image of the god has long since disappeared. However, in this "house of god" one's reward is the journey itself and not the end.

Upon entering the first court, to the left can be seen the chapels to Amon, Mut and Khonsu built by **Sety II** as a way station for the sacred barques. To the right, the mudbrick remains of the ramp, which was used in construction of the pylon, may still be seen. In the southern corner of the court stands a temple built by **Ramesses III** to commemorate his victories. The temple contains no shrine but has rooms that were meant to house the sacred barques. The next pylon, which was rebuilt in Ptolemaic times, leads to the great hypostyle hall built by **Sety I** and completed by his son, Ramesses II. This is beyond all doubt, one of the major achievements of Egyptian architecture. It consists of 12 columns flanking a processional way standing to a height of 70 ft. and an additional 122 columns 43 ft. in height in 7 rows on either side. This papyrus thicket expressed in stone, shows its open capitals at the center of the hall where light would enter from the above clerestory, whereas the capitals of columns more removed where darkness prevailed, remain closed. The columns contain the names of the kings, inscribed at times one over the other; many usurped by Ramesses II. The third pylon was built by **Amenhotep III** in the 18th dynasty and was inlaid with gold and silver from top to bottom as it is recorded. One will need some imagination to visualize this today in it's current condition. Moving farther along and retreating back in time the fourth pylon constructed by **Tuthmosis I** can be seen. This area between the 3rd and 4th pylons has been referred to as the 'court of the obelisks' as several once stood here. This also is the intersection of the two main axes of the temple. The two remaining obelisks in the temple stand here, one by Tuthmosis I on the right and the other to the left by Queen **Hatshepsut**. The plinths (a base that the obelisk sits on), of two others, erected by **Tuthmosis III** also remain. The inscription at the base of the Hatshepsut obelisk records that it took only seven months to cut it at Aswan and erect it here. Additionally it states that it once was covered from top to bottom with electrum, a combination of gold and silver.

Beyond the fifth pylon, built by Tuthmosis I stands the original sanctuary of the temple. His grandson, Tuthmosis III, who built the small sixth pylon, made some alterations to the sanctuary. Carved on the sixth pylon are the names of the towns and villages that Tuthmosis III overcame in Syria, Palestine, and Lebanon.

The central chapel is built of massive granite blocks whose final stage dates from the time of **Philip III Arrhidaeus**, the half brother and successor to **Alexander the Great.** The two sections of the chapel are a vestibule to the west and a shrine proper where the very well preserved central pedestal survives. The barque of the god Amen-Re rested in this spot when not on the move. The various wall reliefs show the king making offerings to the god in his two common forms, one as a walking king and the other as the ithyphallic and mummiform Kamutef. Additionally, scenes from the "Beautiful Feast of the Valley" which took place across the river on the west bank and required that the family of Karnak travel there, can be seen. Behind the sanctuary is a building referred to as the "Festival Hall of Tuthmosis III" built to celebrate his victories in the north. At the rear of this edifice is a small room of interest as it contains representations of the plants and animals brought back to Egypt by this king. The

Kings names you may find at Karnak Temples

Senworset I Kheperkare 1971-1926

Ramesses II (meryamon) Usermatra Setepenre 1279-1212

Seti II (merenptah) Userkheperure-Setepenre 1199-1193

Ramesses III (hekaiunu) Usermaatre Meryamon 1182-1151

Seti I (meryenptah) Menmaatre 1291-1278

Amonhotep III (hekawaset) Nebmaatre 1368-1349

delicacy of detail here should not be missed and some have referred to this as the worlds first zoo.

The north-south axis of Karnak contains mostly a series of pylons and courts; the seventh pylon built by Tuthmosis III and the eighth and ninth built by Hatshepsut and **Horemheb** in that order. The tenth pylon, which was begun by Amenhotep III and completed by Horemheb, marks the southern extent of the precinct of Amon and leads to the temple of Mut, wife of the great god. The temple was built by Amenhotep III and is now, unfortunately, in a state of ruin but worth the walk for the determined adventurer.

Draw the names and identify other rulers you may find.

Tuthmosis I Akheperkare 1518-1504

Queen Hatshepsut Maatkare 1498-1483

Tuthmosis III Menkheperre 1504-1450

Philip III Arrhidaeus Meryamon Setepenre 323-317

Alexander the Great Meryamon Setepenre 332-323

Horemheb (Meryamon) Djeserkheperure 1321-1293

The text of Hatshepsut's Obelisk at Karnak – West Face

The inscriptions here are found on the west face of Hatshepsut's Obelisk standing at Karnak between the Fourth and Fifth Pylons. You may already recognize many of the sign groups. Fill in what you can in the space below. We'll fill in the rest.

West Face

Line 1 (_____) Wsrtkaw (_____) Fresh (or Flourishing) in Years (_____-_____)

Divine of Risings (_____) (_____)

Line 2 She made (it) as her monument for her father (_____) (_____) of the thrones of

the (_____)

Line 3 Erecting for him two great obelisks at the august gate: " (_____) is Great in Terror"

Line 4 With very much electrum which illuminate the (_____) like the sun. Never was...

Line 5 the like made since the beginning. May the (_____), Khnm(t)-Amon, Hatshepsut,

perform (_____).

The sign group within the serekh (line one) represents Wsrtkaw, Mighty or Powerful of Kas.

The text of Hatshepsut's Obelisk at Karnak – North Face

The inscriptions here are found on the north face of Hatshepsut's Obelisk standing at Karnak between the Fourth and Fifth Pylons. You may already recognize many of the sign groups. Fill in what you can in the space below.

North Face

Line 1 (_____) (_____) (_____),

Fresh (or Flourishing) in Years, Divine of Risings, (_____)

(_____) (_____).

Line 2 Her father (_____) has established her great name (_____) upon the august Ished tree;

Line 3 moreover, her annals are millions of years united with (_____).

Line 4 (_____) Khnm(t)-Amen, Hatshepsut, beloved of (_____)

king of the gods, heir to this beautiful, stone carved monument.

Line 5 (When) she celebrated for him the first occurrence of the Heb-sed festival (so that) she may do

(_____).

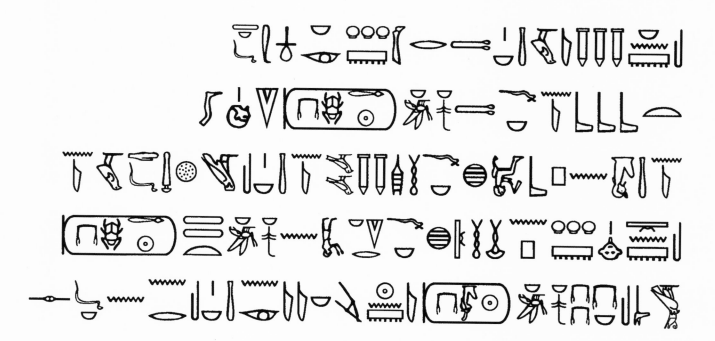

The text of Hatshepsut's Obelisk at Karnak – East Face

The inscriptions here are found on the east face of Hatshepsut's Obelisk standing at Karnak between the Fourth and Fifth Pylons. You may already recognize many of the sign groups. Fill in what you can in the space below.

East Face

Line 1 (_____) (_____) (_____)

(_____) beloved of (_____). Her majesty made the name of her father

Line 2 established upon this monument, enduring, when favor was given to the (_____),

(_____), Akheperkare, (Tuthmosis I).

Line 3 by the majesty of this august god, when the two great (_____) were erected by her majesty
on the first occasion (of jubilee)

Line 4 the (_____) of the gods said: Indeed, your father, king of (_____),

(_____) gave 'command' (placed under the foot?)

Line 5 to erect (_____), and your majesty will repeat the monuments (so that) you may do.
May she live forever.

The text of Hatshepsut's Obelisk at Karnak – South Face

The inscriptions here are found on the south face of Hatshepsut's Obelisk standing at Karnak between the Fourth and Fifth Pylons. You may already recognize many of the sign groups. Fill in what you can in the space below.

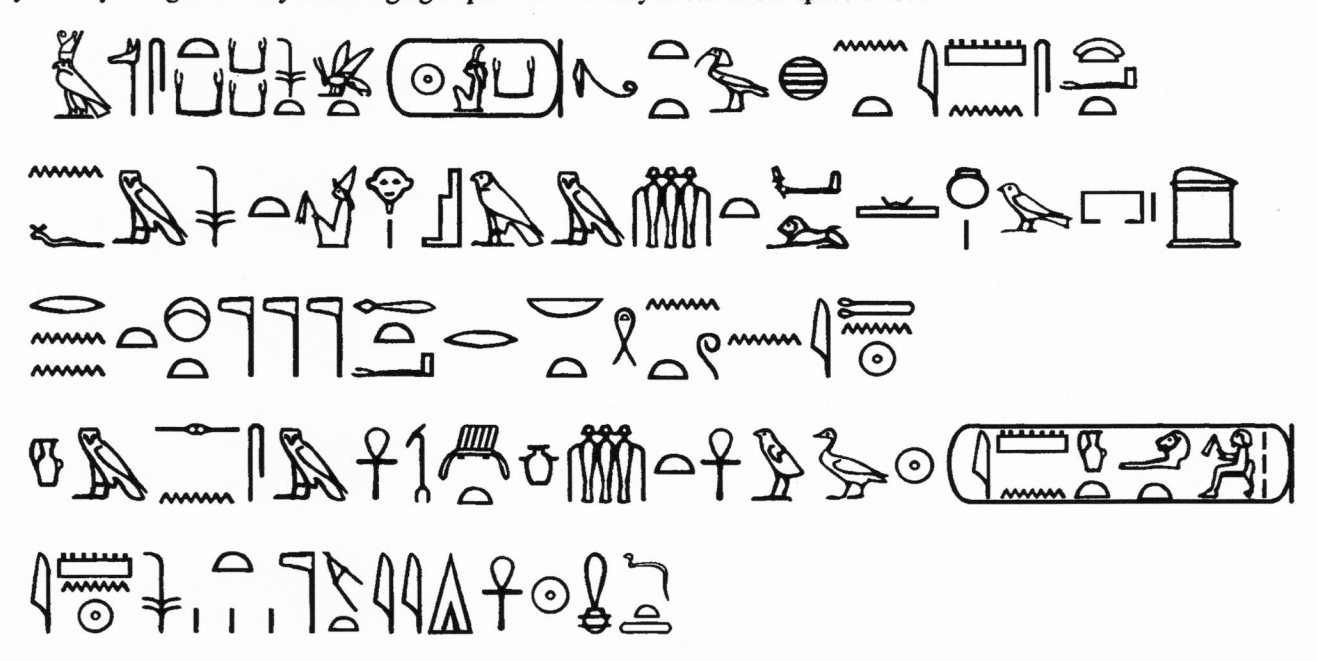

South Face

Line 1 (_____) (_____) (_____)

(_____) the glorious image of (_____), whom he has caused to appear

Line 2 as king upon the throne of (_____) in the face of the splendors of the great house, whom

Line 3 the great ennead of gods has brought up to be mistress of the circuit of the sun.

Line 4 They have united her with life, satisfaction and joy in front of the living (_____)

(_____) (_____),

Line 5 beloved of (_____), king of the gods, (_____).

Middle Egypt: a Delightful Side Trip

The area roughly to the south of the Faiyum and north of Luxor is generally referred to as Middle Egypt. This especially refers to the area around Beni Hassan and Tell el-Amarna, the location where the so-called heretic Pharaoh, Akhenaten, came to build his city, dedicated to the god Aten (the disk of the sun), in the Eighteenth Dynasty.

Today, little remains of his city that lasted for only a few years and was abandoned after his reign as the court moved back to Thebes, the traditional southern capitol.

The tombs at Beni Hassan belonged to Middle Kingdom nomarchs: local governors who frequently took royal prerogatives unto themselves during the Intermediate periods. The coffins of these local "strong men" reflect spells and titles usually reserved only for royalty. Their tombs are situated along a cliff side terrace on the east bank of the Nile. The most famous of these is the tomb of Khnumhotep which shows the traders bringing their goods in a caravan, gardening scenes and a tree full of birds. Unfortunately, for the last several years, tours have regularly avoided this locale due to civil unrest in the area.

A bit farther south and accessible from Luxor, are the temples of Dendera and Abydos. These are the topic of the next section presented here. Both are well worth the day-trip that one needs to take in these structures. An early departure from Luxor will allow both to be seen in a single day. Each has a unique aspect to recommend it; Dendera with its zodiac ceiling and stairway processions of priests leading to the roof, and Abydos with its famous king list.

The countryside that one travels through is one of sugar cane fields and small villages that give a flavor of local life. Smoke can usually be seen rising from the fields since the farmers are either burning their fields in order to clear them, or the cane is being boiled down in the refining process. Small gauge railways with sugar cane trains can often be seen, as this is how the raw cane is usually moved out of the fields. Sugar cane fields can be seen throughout the vicinity of Luxor, as it is a major cash crop for the area unlike the crops which were grown during the pharaonic period which were of a subsistence nature (i.e. barley, onions and emmer wheat).

The Temple of Hathor at Dendera

The Temple of Hathor at Dendera stands on the west bank of the Nile opposite the town of Qena about 40 miles north of Luxor. The town itself was important from as far back as Old Kingdom times, but none of the presently visible structures date from before 350 BCE. The main temple which was started by **Ptolemy XII** (80-51 BCE) and continued in construction until the time of Nero (54-68 CE), has remained unfinished.

The Emperor Domitian constructed the outer enclosure wall and its gateway in the first century CE. The eighteen columns of the pronaos proper, and an additional six, through which one enters the structure today, are in the form of a sistrum. This instrument is associated with the goddess who also has her cow-like head reproduced on the capitals. Above, the astronomical ceiling is decorated with the daily journey of the sun, the lunar cycle, the 12 hours of the day and night and the signs of the zodiac. On the walls the body of the sky-goddess Nut can be seen swallowing the sun disc in the evening and giving new birth to it in the morning. The hypostyle hall is flanked by a series of rooms where offerings were received. Walking through this hall to the next columned, but smaller hall, a door to the right leads to a staircase to the roof. The walls of this staircase are carved with reliefs depicting the priests ascending to the roof in the *Festival of the New Year*. The king is seen being followed by the priests carrying various symbols and the portable chapels. Here on the roof was the *Court of the New Year* and *The Pure Place* which every temple possessed. The twelve columns of the roof chapel had their faces turned to the four cardinal directions. The statues of the gods were exposed to the sun's rays and thus re-charged for another year. On the columns can be seen the hippopotamus-goddess representing the twelve months of the year. The opposite staircase shows the return trip.

Turning our attention to the six chapels located here on the roof in two groups of three, we find that these are dedicated to the resurrection of Osiris. The purpose of these chapels was to guarantee the annual resurrection of the chthonic deity during a festival held as the waters of the Nile receded following the annual flood. This ritual, as described on the walls of the chapel, indicates that a paste replica of the god was made mostly from barley, watered and allowed to germinate. It was later buried in one of the chapels. This has parallels in what is termed the *Corn Osiris* which may be found in tombs in Egypt. Here the germinating god gives new life to the body of the deceased as it grows in the confines of the tomb. Protecting spirits that were invoked during this ritual can be seen on the walls of the chapels. It is also of note that one of these chapels contained the famous zodiac that is now reproduced in plaster here, the original having been removed

The Temple of Hathor at Dendera, night.

to the Louvre in France.

Returning to the small columned hall, one then proceeds to the central shrine or sanctuary of the temple. The granite naos which once contained the statue of the goddess is, sadly, no longer there. This sanctuary also contained the barques of Hathor, Horus, Isis and Harsomtus that can be seen on the walls. Surrounding the sanctuary and separating it from the rest of the temple and the outside are a series of eleven chapels. These are dedicated to (from the left facing the sanctuary) Hathor, Isis, Sokar, Harsomtus, four more to Hathor, Horus of Edfu, and two more to Hathor.

Beyond the sanctuary in a side chamber is one of the temple crypts. It is believed that here many of the temple treasures were kept. The walls of this small crypt are lined with excellent reliefs of some of these objects. Here, an inscription on the wall tells that the first temple on this site was of predynastic date and the records of this are said to have been written on leather when the present temple was built.

On the outer wall in back of the temple are reliefs showing offerings being made to the goddess by **Cleopatra VII.** This is one of the few depictions showing her. Standing in front of her in traditional pharaonic dress is her son by Julius Caesar, **Caesarion.**

Close to the entrance to the temple stand two 'mamissi' or birth houses. The first dates from the time of **Nectanebo** (380-363 BCE.) and is the oldest structure on the site. The second is in an unfinished state and bears the cartouches of Trajan and Antoninus Pius. Both are dedicated to Harsomtus,

the son of Hathor and Horus. The scenes that decorate the south wall where a fifth century Coptic basilica was built are of exceptional quality and show extraordinary detail. They are truly worth a look.

Ptolemy XII (Neos Dionysos)
Iwaenpanetjernehem Setepptah Irmaat
80-58, 55-51

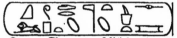

Queen Cleopatra VII (netjeret-merites)
51-30

Ptolemy XV Caesarion
Iwapanetjer entynehem Setepenptah
Irmaatenre Sekhemankhamun 36-30

Abydos: Holy Since the Beginning of Egyptian History

The Temple at Abydos built by Sety I, who ruled between 1305 and 1290 BCE, was started towards the beginning of his reign and not completed until after his death by his son Ramesses II. It shows three different styles of building in its completed form. The main building and part of the south wing can be dated to the time of Sety I and show decoration in one style. The First and Second courts, a small esplanade at the temple's rear, the Corridor of the Bull and Hall of Barques belong to the second phase completed by Ramesses II immediately following the death of Sety I. The third phase, also completed by Ramesses II, is seen in the First Hypostyle Hall along with evidence showing the over-cutting of the name of Sety by Ramesses.

Mythologically speaking, Seti I's temple, like all others, was representative of the original mound of creation and included most of the architectural features found at other temples: forecourts, hypostyle halls, sanctuary area and storerooms. The rituals performed at Abydos were similar in nature to those carried out at all other temples in Egypt with the exception of the Osiris Rituals. When one regards the overall plan of the temple and its attendant structure, it seems to form a unit architecturally and mythologically and was designed that way.

The design of the temple differs in several ways from that which is usually seen in Egyptian temples. The temple is not built on one main axis, as in standard temple form. The L-shape of the Abydos temple shows a departure from the norm and is, in fact, unique in Egyptian temple architecture. There have been several theories put forward to explain this, but none seem satisfactory. One popular explanation for this design abated to the adjoining unique structure on the site: the Osirion. It may be that these two structures were part of a single plan with the temple constructed to link with the Osirion, the supposed burial place of the god Osiris. There is also evidence here of a structure that was, perhaps, a storage area with an attached hall for the receiving of gifts or tribute.

Another major departure is evidenced in the number of shrines seen here. It would be usual to have only one shrine in a temple, dedicated to the major god and perhaps some smaller side chapels for subsidiary deities such as a consort or son. At Abydos, we find no less than seven main shrines in the sanctuary area, which are dedicated to two main triads; the imperial Ramesside gods and the Osirian family. Additionally there is one shrine dedicated to the dead and deified Sety I. This original design may owe its genesis of form to a desire to symbolize reconciliation in the land following the conflict of the Amarna period. At Abydos, as at other Egyptian temples, a wealth of evidence exists to show that the layout and design of the temple was never an occasional thing, but followed a specific plan grounded in ritual purpose.

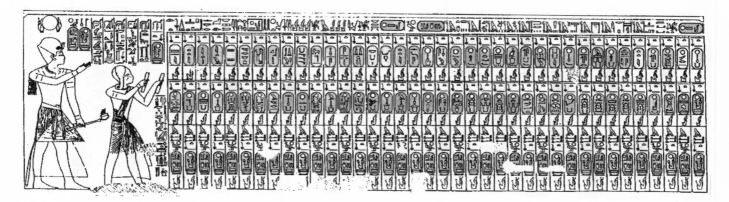

Find and name these kings on the famous King Table at Abydos.

_____

_____

_____

_____

_____

_____

The Valley of the Kings and the Mansions of Millions of Years

The royal necropolis of Thebes, which today is known as the Valley of the Kings, was in ancient times called The Great Place. The royal burial procession would make its way from the mortuary temples at the edge of the flood plain, over the cliffs and down into the valley. This route follows the western passage of the sun into the Valley of the Kings behind the western horizon. As such, this passage incorporates the king into the solar cycle and here the pharaoh would join the entourage of the god Re in his continuing journey of death and rebirth.

There are two natural features that make this site perhaps a more suitable place than others for the royal burial. The first is the natural pyramid that rises over this valley. This peak was thought to be a gate of heaven and was inhabited by Hathor and later the goddess Meretseger, or She Who Loves Silence, and who can be seen as She Who Faces Her Lord, Amon, at Karnak. The second significant feature is the *akhet* or glyph for *horizon* ☉ , that is formed by the cliffs here. This, no doubt, made the area especially meaningful and quite well placed for the royal necropolis.

Measures had to be taken to ensure the continued existence of the royal *ka* and *ba* and the other aspects of the soul. This was necessary for the continued well being of the cosmos itself. The ancient Egyptians were perhaps the first people to attempt to make guides to the "other side" and they placed them on the walls of their king's tombs or *Mansions of Millions of Years* as they referred to the tombs.

Today, the visitor can see the amazing result of their developing thought of the world beyond displayed in these tombs. Not only were the walls decorated with that which one would need to know for successful navigation to the next world, but the tomb architecture itself is a reflection of these changing ideas of the pathways of Re. Each tomb is a unique experience, as no two are exactly alike in decoration or structure. We can say that over the course of the years three major types of tomb design are visible and they reflect these changing attitudes. This development corresponds roughly to the 18th, 19th and 20th dynasties with some overlap.

Here we will follow the terminology as laid out by Egyptologist Richard Wilkinson of the University of Arizona Egyptian Expedition in referring to those of the 18th dynasty as *bent axis* of the 19th as *jogged axis* and the 20th as *straight axis*. The use of this terminology will become immediately apparent to the visitor in the valley. Erik Hornung, a German Egyptologist, has stated in reference to the design of 18th dynasty tombs, "The architecture of the tomb is thus conditioned by the topography of the Beyond, while the texts and representations frequently take up the theme of the bent or winding waters in the landscape of the realm of the dead."

18th Dynasty tombs

The early 18th dynasty tombs have a series of passageways that have either steps or ramps (sometimes alternating), leading down to the first chamber, called alternatively the *hall of waiting* or the *hall of hindrance*. Continuing on, a small pillared hall is encountered which leads to a second pillared hall called *the house of gold*. Here the royal burial was placed. The symbolic entrance to 18th dynasty tombs was regarded to be in the south, with the burial chamber in the north, notwithstanding the actual orientation. The suggestion in this design is the nocturnal journey of the sun under the earth.

The design details of the 18th dynasty burial chambers are perhaps less well understood than is commonly believed. Some of the earliest show an oval shape and so may be linked to the royal cartouche shape. Also of note is the fact that some royal sarcophagi show this shape. An open papyrus scroll has also been put forward as a shape for consideration and one must admit to this possibility as wall decorations reflect this in their color and inscriptional styles. The royal tombs of this period (18th dynasty) usually show scenes from the Book of the Amduat or, "That which is in the Netherworld", referred to by the Egyptians as The Book of the Secret Chambers. In the tomb of **Tuthmosis III (KV 34)**, the Litany of Re can also be seen. Two tombs of note from this period are that of Tuthmosis III and of **Tutankhamon (KV 62)**.

The Tuthmosis III tomb is of particular interest due to the fine rendering in early style of the Book of the Amduat in the burial chamber along with the Litany of Re on the pillars in this room. This tomb shows a complete copy of the Amduat and is the only one, with the exception of Amenhotep II to do so. Additionally, this is the first tomb to show the Litany of Re which would become used in many tombs following Sety I in the 19th dynasty. The winding nature of the architecture here is a classic example of the style in this period. The tomb of Tutankhamon is addressed in another section of this book.

19th Dynasty tombs

Beginning in the 19th dynasty there is noticeable change in the tombs of the valley. The bent-axis design of the 18th dynasty is now abandoned for the jogged-axis design seen from the tomb of Horemheb on. There is additionally a movement from the underworld books to an emphasis on the solar cycle in the decoration. The descent angle of the tombs is also less steep with doors now being used in place of sealed and hidden entrances. This may be an indication that the tombs were now being regularly opened for inspection purposes or for festivals. Access to side-rooms, which now seems to increase in number, is through wooden doors in place of the sealed ones of the preceding dynasty. Wilkinson has pointed out that these changes perhaps indicate more than simply a structural variation. The indication here is one of an introduction, which is architectural in nature, of new symbolic features that incorporate the above-mentioned solar cycle. The orientation of the tomb now moves from one of a north-south direction as seen in the 18th dynasty to an east-west axis. This would of course reflect the path of the sun on its daily journey to the underworld and the west-east return path.

The moving of the Litany of Re from the inner depths of the tomb to the entranceway at this time also underscores this basic theological change observed in tomb design. From the time of **Ramesses II (KV 7)** forward, one can see the tripartite representation of the sun god in his forms as the beetle Khepri (the morning sun), and the ram-headed Atum (the evening manifestation), inscribed upon the disk of Re, the mid-day sun, over the entrance to the tomb. The symbolic significance of this, in this writer's opinion, is quite far reaching in that what we may well be observing here is an early example of the idea of the 'Om' as manifest in other oriental traditions.

It is often pointed out that this is the *four-syllable element* and an expression of the nature of the cosmos. It is explained that the opening syllable is the *coming into being*, the next is the *filling of the mouth* in the fullness of the form, and lastly the *closing off* of the sound. The fourth element is called the *silence* from which it comes and to which it goes back. Here at the tomb entrance we see the god Khepri, whose name in ancient Egyptian is the verb meaning *to come into being*, followed by the sun-disk itself in the fullness of the day, and lastly the ram-headed Atum who represents the closing off of the cycle. The fourth element, that of the silence, would of course, be the tomb itself. It is the silence out of which one comes, as indicated by the Egyptian Book of the Dead, or as they called it, The Book of the Coming Forth by Day and that same silence to which the soul returns at night.

It is also interesting to note that almost all the representations of the solar disk within the tomb are in a deep red color that is indicative of the sun's evening and night appearance. Perhaps the single exception to this iconography is the sun when seen being re-born between the thighs of the sky goddess Nut. Here it is shown as a golden winged disk but, in keeping with the symbolism, the sun disk is shown as red before she swallows it and while it passes through her body.

If additional justification of this new orientation of the tomb were needed, one need only look at the representations of the goddesses Isis and Nephthys, who are symbolically associated with the south and north respectively, in their position flanking the sun-disk at the tomb entrance. The use of the flora of Upper (southern) and Lower (northern) Egypt at the tomb entrance give additional indication. This then gives us a complete north-south and east-west orientation for the tomb.

Moving into the tomb it will be noticed that the front part of the 19th dynasty tomb is dedicated to images of a solar nature while at the first pillared hall, the usual point of the axis jog, the images take on a representation of the Osirian realm. This shows a symbolic equating of the front half of the tomb with the symbolic east and the back being the symbolic west. The image of Re may be seen in the back half of the tomb, but he takes second place in importance and size to Osiris.

There seems to be more regularity in positioning of the royal sarcophagi of this period in that they all seem to be oriented with the head to the north. This would be a reflection of the ancient idea of the king joining the 'imperishable stars', the ones that never set, in the northern sky, just as his ancestors did in the pyramid age. This orientation would also mean that they faced the south, which was their cardinal direction, just as the north is ours.

Two 19th dynasty tombs of note are the tombs of **Ramesses I (KV 16)** and the transitional tomb of **Horemheb (KV 57)**. The tomb of Ramesses I is small because of his short reign. The painted scenes of the Book of Gates are some of the finest to be seen. The funerary chamber is also decorated with the king shown in the presence of the various gods. The tomb of Horemheb shows the decorative motif in various stages of work done by very skillful artists. The use of color is quite noticeable in this tomb with the use of multicolored hieroglyphs on a blue-gray background. Here the Book of Gates was used for the first time in place of the Amduat in the burial chamber. This tomb is a good example of the jogged-axis type with long corridors of a rather steep nature. Unfinished walls are evident with the decoration in the burial chamber only partly complete as time evidently ran out.

20th Dynasty tombs

The 20th Dynasty is a time of simplification and, with a few exceptions (esp. Ramesses VI), one of reduction in tomb size. Further developments in symbolism in the royal tombs also are manifest at this time. The king takes on a direct association with the solar deity and can be seen joined with him in both his diurnal and nocturnal journeys. This can be very graphically seen in the tomb of **Ramesses IV (KV 2),** as the kings full, formal titulary can be seen inscribed along the center of the ceiling in the hall leading to the burial chamber. The royal name, then, symbolically follows the path of the sun on it's journey, with the cartouche taking the place of the sun disk as was seen in temple ceilings and entrances.

Starting in the tomb of **Ramesses III (KV 11)**, the orientation of the sarcophagus was redirected to align along the main axis (east-west) of the tomb. The head of the king was placed in the west end of the tomb so that the mummy always looked towards the east, symbolically at least, and towards the rising sun. One can hardly miss the significance of this orientation, as the king is therefore re-born with the rising of the sun everyday.

Additionally, in the royal tombs of this period, the sky-goddess Nut can be seen on the ceiling of the burial chamber. Her orientation may give rise to question however, as she is seen swallowing the evening sun in the direction of the entrance (the east). This would seem to be the reverse of the architectural and design program of the tomb. Wilkinson has pointed out that it may, in fact, have been felt that it was more important to have the point of re-birth, (i.e. the emergence of the solar disk from between her thighs as she gives it new life every morning), over the head of the king. Her depiction on the inside of the Ramesside period sarcophagi lids continues however, to be with her head to the west (at the head of the mummy) as would be expected.

Along with the image of the goddess Nut, the ceilings were also decorated with the Book of the Day and Book of the Night. Of additional note is the fact that nothing can be seen to the outside of the over-arching body of the goddess where one might expect to see stars or other deities shown. One explanation for this may be that the goddess encloses all of creation under her body, and as such there would be no existence beyond the limits of her body.

Among the tomb plans that have come down to us from the ancient Egyptians is that of **Ramesses VI (KV 9)**. This plan names the different parts of the tomb and thus gives us further insight into tomb planning in the Late New Kingdom. The corridors themselves are referred to as The Places Where the God was Dragged. This is surely in reference to the ledge upon which the royal mummy was laid and taken to the burial chamber. These passages were decorated with scenes from the Book of Gates on the left, and the Book of Caverns on the right with astronomical ceilings in each corridor. In this instance, the Book of Caverns has replaced The Litany of Re. In the well room and first pillared hall, the books of Gates, Caverns, and Heavens are depicted. Farther along, in the lower corridors, scenes from the Books of the Heavens are seen on the ceiling and the Book of the Amduat appears on the walls. The next area indicated is The Hall for Final Rites or the antechamber, where the king is seen before various deities and additionally shows scenes from the spells of the Book of the Dead. Beyond this is the sarcophagus chamber with scenes from the Book of the Earth (Aker) and the Nut ceiling. This is one of the longest tombs in the valley, measuring approximately 310 ft. in length and it contains complete versions of many of the above mentioned books. These books are, in fact, real books and not just a collection of spells like the Pyramid Texts or the Book of the Dead. The theme of these compositions is that life and death are a continuous process, that life engenders death and in death, there is new life.

All of the royal Theban religious literature deals with life, death and the resurrection of the sun god. The son of the sun, the pharaoh, has his fate linked with this god. Tombs of this period to be viewed, if accessible, are the above-mentioned one of Ramesses VI or **Ramesses IX (KV 6)** which is the first tomb on the route. It contains many rooms decorated with scenes from the sacred books of this period along with the astronomical images on the ceiling. Many tombs of the Ramesside period will show the astronomical ceiling with the goddess Nut and at least portions of the named compositions on their walls. This points to an increased attention to the solar aspects of religious thought manifest in the 20th dynasty.

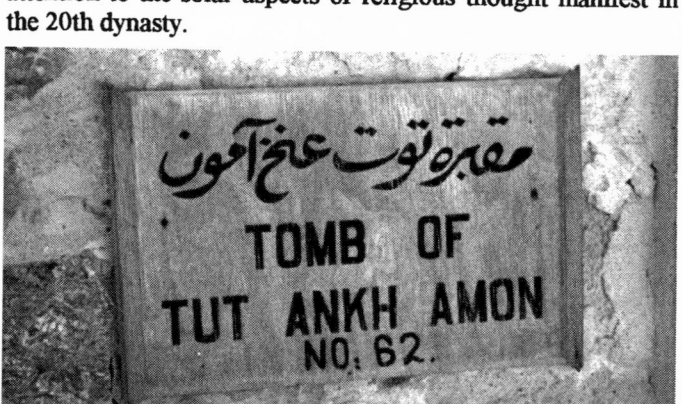

Greeters of the Sun: Baboons in the First Hour of the Amduat

An interesting feature of the burial chamber of Tutankhamon is the twelve baboons that appear on the west wall. This scene, taken as a whole composition, is representative of the "First Hour of the Amduat" from the "Book of the Amduat". When comparing the overall size of this tomb in contrast with others in the Valley of the Kings, it is clear why the need for consolidation was felt necessary. This is a good example of the Egyptian sense of "pars pro toto", or a part being representative for all.

The scene shows the gateway into the unknown of the Netherworld. In this hour, the solar baboons rejoice upon seeing the sun god at the gates of the Netherworld. Here, in the developing religious thought of the New Kingdom, the king is intimately connected with the sun god in his travel towards a "rebirth" at dawn. The scarab beetle in the solar barque, the morning form of the god, already being worshipped, prefigures the successful completion of this journey by Osiris in the register above. Uppermost is the glyph for "heaven" stretching across the entire scene with a row of glyphs beneath. The reference in this corrupt text is to the god Re entering into the Great City (the Netherworld). Below this and preceding the solar barque are a series of five deities named from right to left as Ma'at, the Lady of the Barque, Horus, Ka-shu, and Nehes.

The baboons that make up the remaining part of the west wall are all named, although these names are somewhat enigmatic in nature. That the baboons should be the first guardians encountered at the entrance is no accident. The Egyptians undoubtedly observed their morning antics as they jump and chatter at the rising sun. Here in the first hour, they sing to Re and open the doors to the Netherworld. We will give only a transcription with a comment on these. It will be obvious that the glyphs before the apes are both red and black in color and some feel that the black represents an older version of the name.

Reading right to left and in rows across, top to bottom:

1. ib-t3, perhaps "The Heart of the Land"
2. bntj, "2 Baboons"
3. hkn-m-bs-f, "Praise to His Secret (Form?)"
4. httj, "Ape"
5. ib-ib-t3, "Favorite of the Land"
6. ifw (perhaps iwf), "Flesh" a name given to the sun god in the Amduat.
7. ib3w, "The Dancer"
8. p3tt, an old designation for baboon.
9. iknw, "Water Drawer"?
10. dhdh, a kind of ape, name of a protector god of Osiris in the Book of the Dead.
11. name missing.
12. bsy, "Secret Image", the name of the sun god.

The Tombs in the Valley of the Kings

Undated: Open in antiquity before formal archaeology

KV 1	Ramesses VII	
KV 2	Ramesses IV	
KV 3	son of Ramesses III	
KV 4	Ramesses XI	
KV 5	sons of Ramesses II	
KV 6	Ramesses IX	
KV 7	Ramesses II	
KV 8	Merenptah	
KV 9	Ramesses V & VI	
KV 10	Amenmesses	
KV 11	Ramesses III	
KV 12	anonymous royal family	
KV 13	Bay, a chancellor	
KV 14	Twosret/ Seti II (?)/ Setnakht	
KV 15	Seti II	

Most shown with date of discovery

KV 16	Ramesses I	1817
KV 17	Seti I	1817
KV 18	Ramesses X	
KV 19	Ramesses Montuhirkopeshef (Ramesses VIII ?)	1817
KV 20	Tuthmose I and Hatshepsut	1799
KV 21	Two queens of Dynasty XVIII	1817
WV 22	Amenhotep III	1799
WV 23	Aye (originally Tutankhamon)	1816
WV 24	anonymous	
WV 25	Possibly Akhenaten's original tomb	1814
KV 26		1898
KV 27	Family tomb Dynasty XVIII	1898
KV 28		1898
KV 29		1899
KV 30	Family tomb Dynasty XVIII	1817
KV 31		1817
KV 32		1898
KV 33		1898
KV 34	Tuthmosis III	1898
KV 35	Amenhotep II	1898
KV 36	Mahirpra	1899
KV 37	anonymous	1899
KV 38	Tuthmosis I relocated by Tuthmosis III from KV 20	1899
KV 39	Amenhotep I (?)	1899
KV 40	anonymous	1899
KV 41	anonymous	1899
KV 42	Hatshepsut-Merytre wife of Tuthmosis III	1900
KV 43	Tuthmosis IV	1903
KV 44	Dynasty XVIII but containing Tentkaru of Dynasty XXII	1901
KV 45	Userhet	1902
KV 46	Yuya & Tuya	1905
KV 47	Siptah	1905
KV 48	Vizir Amenemopet	1906
KV 49	Dynasty XVIII (?)	1906
KV 50-52	Animal burials	1906
KV 53		1905-6
KV 54	Tutankhamon cache	1907
KV 55	Amarna cache -Tiye & Akhenaten (?)	1907
KV 56	A Jewelry cache	1908
KV 57	Horemheb	1908
KV 58		1909
KV 59	Unfinished pit	
KV 60	Sitre-in & Hatshepsut (?)	1903
KV 61		1903
KV 62	Tutankhamon (originally Aye)	1922

KV = Kings Valley, WV= Western Valley

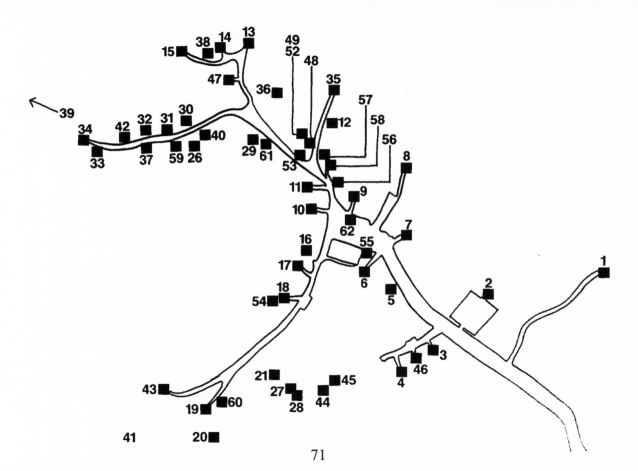

The Valley of the Queens: *Ta-set-neferu*, The Place of Beauty

The term *Valley of the Queens* was first used by Jean Francois Champollion in the 19th century of the common era. There are eighty numbered tombs in the valley but only about twenty are decorated and of this number only a few are open to the public. Many of the tombs are really not much more than pit graves of which we know very little. The oldest date from the Eighteenth Dynasty and seem to be of an anonymous nature. It is only with the coming of the Nineteenth Dynasty that queens and the royal children begin to be buried in this rather desolate valley which the ancients called "the place of the beauteous ones." For the next two hundred years it was the final stop for many important members of the court, most importantly those of kings Ramesses II and Ramesses III.

The valley contains some very important and famous queens of the Nineteenth Dynasty such as Sat-re, the wife of Ramesses I; Mut-tuy, the wife of Sety I; and most notably Nefertari, favorite of Ramesses II. In several cases these tombs contain selections from chapters of the Book of the Dead. This is due to the fact that these burials were not of a sovereign or king, but rather of wives and children. As such, the choice of textual tomb decoration was limited in nature. These texts or spells were designed to guide the dead on the journey to the beyond and it was not necessary to have all the nearly two hundred texts inscribed to be considered efficacious.

The tomb of **Queen Tyti (QV52)** is one of the finest in the valley, but also is one of the most mysterious, as the tomb does not record with which king she is to be associated. Speculation is that she is one of the wives of a 20th Dynasty king, perhaps Ramesses III and perhaps the mother of Ramesses IV. She is depicted in the tomb with sidelocks indicating a youthful visage. We see her in the company of several gods and goddesses including Ptah, Thoth, Atum, Isis and Nephthys in the entrance corridor. Moving into the second chamber, which has two rooms to either side, the queen is seen in various activities. In the right-hand chamber the queen is seen making an offering to the goddess Hathor who is shown in her bovine form and emerging from the sacred mountain. To the left she is seen as Iunmutef (literally the pillar of his mother), and represents the young Horus. In the last chamber Osiris is seen between Neith and Selket along with Nephthys and Thoth. Here offerings would be placed before the gods.

The tomb of **Amonherkhopshef (QV 55)** is that of a son of Pharaoh Ramesses III. A crown prince, who died in childhood and was buried in the valley, he is shown being led by his father to the gods in the first hall. The well-preserved scenes in this tomb are among the best in either the Valley of the Kings or Queens. The king is seen greeting Duamutef with his young son dutifully following behind his father and also offering incense. The young prince is additionally seen being greeted by Ptah-Tenen with his father in the next world. These scenes of Ramesses III leading his young son in introduction to the gods are among the most *human* to be found in any of the royal tombs and help us link to these ancient people. In the passage following, scenes from chapter 146 of the Book of the Dead can be seen.

Depicted here are portals five through eight of the twenty-one portals, perhaps with the idea of *pars pro toto*, to the domain of Osiris. It was considered crucial that the deceased have knowledge and be able to name the portal and it's keeper who would attempt to block successful passage.

Perhaps, however, the most famous of the tombs in the Valley of the Queens, is that of **Queen Nefertari (QV66)** the favorite consort of Ramesses II.

The tomb was discovered in 1904 by the Italian archaeologist Ernesto Schiaparelli who was the leader of the Italian Archaeological Mission in Egypt from 1903 to 1920. The tomb itself consists of an entrance hall with recesses to the right leading to a side chamber. Returning to the entrance hall, a descending passage leads to a pillared sarcophagus chamber with three additional side chambers. The halls, chambers, passage and pillars are decorated throughout with scenes of the gods and their recitations, and portions of chapters 17, 94, 144, 146, and 148 of the Book of the Dead.

The entrance chamber is almost a square measuring 5 x 5.2 meters. Upon entering, to the left can be seen depictions and inscriptions from chapter 17 of the Book of the Dead. This is one of the longer chapters and among the oldest. It has a multi-purpose function for the deceased. First it speaks of the identity of Re and Atum and then continues in a much more esoteric way to help the deceased, the queen in this case,

go forth, to quote the rubric of the chapter, *as a living soul after she has died.* The illustrations above the text (south wall) begin with the queen seen playing senet, a popular board game of the time, followed by her transformation to a ba bird atop a shrine, her aspect which has the ability to leave the tomb for a short time, and finally the earth god Akeru who is seen on the next (west) wall.

Various scenes continue on the west wall with the *benu* bird (perhaps the phoenix), a bed with the mummy upon it flanked on either side by Nephthys (at the head), and Isis in the form of kites (hawks) as is customary in such scenes.

Following this is an androgynous water god and two rather damaged vignettes. The scroll of the 17th chapter then turns once again and follows to the entryway of the burial chamber. Here there seems to be no correspondence between the vignettes and the text below although the beings all do have a place in the 17th chapter. The two seated mummiform figures at the end and just in advance of the doorway, would seem to represent Re (falcon-headed) and Shu, the form of air and light. Above the door, the four Sons of Horus are seen, and here a mistake on the part of the scribe can be observed. The names of Qebehsenef and Duamutef (the falcon-headed and jackel-headed gods) are exchanged.

Moving to the side chamber, the south wall shows scenes from chapter 148 of the Book of the Dead. The top register contains four cows, the middle three cows and a bull, and the lower shows the four steering oars that help the deceased navigate between the stars. Additionally, each oar is named and has an association with one of the cardinal directions. The text of chapter 148 tells that the cows have the ability to provide for the queen the foodstuffs shown on the offering tables before them: milk, bread and vegetables.

Nefertari can be seen praising them just around on the west wall. The next scene is one of some major theological importance as it shows the syncretism that often occurs with Egyptian gods. Here the ram-headed, mummiform god, who is identified as Re, stands between Isis and Nephthys. The text to left and right reads *"It is Osiris who rests in Re"* and *"It is Re who rests in Osiris."* This shows the polarity and the fusing of the two most important deities for the deceased, showing again that in death there is life by the intermixing of the two.

Moving down the descending corridor to the burial chamber are another collection of goddesses who receive offerings from Nefertari. To the east are Hathor, Selket and Ma'at and on the west wall are Isis, Nephthys and Ma'at. The goddess Ma'at also guards above the entrance to the burial chamber, a line of glyphs above her out-stretched wings reads: "Words spoken by Ma'at, daughter of Re (I) protect (my) daughter, the king's great wife, Nefertari, beloved of Mut, justified." Here the student of the Egyptian language should take note of the interplay between the written word and the image, which is always present in Egyptian calligraphy. Following the word for *protection,* a personal pronoun is needed but none is written. In place of this the artist has chosen to have the feather of the goddess Ma'at project up into the line of glyphs and thus insert the figure of the goddess herself in place of the necessary word.

The burial chamber itself shows texts from chapter 144 of the Book of the Dead to the left, and chapter 146 to the right. Chapter 144 is a description of the gates leading to the realm of Osiris and the queen must have knowledge of their names, as well as the names of the gatekeepers. The Book of the Dead describes seven of these of which five appear in the tomb.

Chapter 146 contains the portals to the Osirian domain and the same idea applies. As before, twenty-one portals are indicated with only ten shown in Nefertari's tomb. This is undoubtedly a case of *pars pro toto*. The gates themselves have three attendants; a keeper, guardian and announcer, while the portals require only a single keeper.

The pillars stand at the corners of the space marked out as the sarcophagus area that rests some 40 cm. below the actual floor. Entering the tomb, the traveler is greeted by the figures of two priests facing the entrance to the burial chamber. To the left is the priest Iunmutef, Pillar of His Mother, and to the right is Horendotes the Avenger of his Father. They both gesture towards the sarcophagus depression.

On the inner sides of these pillars is the image of Osiris in his booth facing the entrance of the tomb to welcome the deceased queen into his realm. The djed pillars are seen facing each other on all four columns and the queen before the various gods and goddesses decorate the remaining. Three small annexes coming off the sarcophagus chamber make up the remaining rooms of this magnificently decorated tomb.

Up the hill behind the souvenir stands is the tomb of **Crown Prince Khaemwaset**, son of Ramesses III. Most of the brilliant murals show the young prince with his father offering to the gods. In the first corridor, the king offers to the deities in the name of his son. In the side rooms, he worships Anubis and the four sons of Horus, while Isis and Nephthys greet Osiris on the back wall. Inscriptions from the Book of Gates are found in the second corridor. In the burial chamber, the king appears to represent his son before Osiris.

The Valley of the Queens

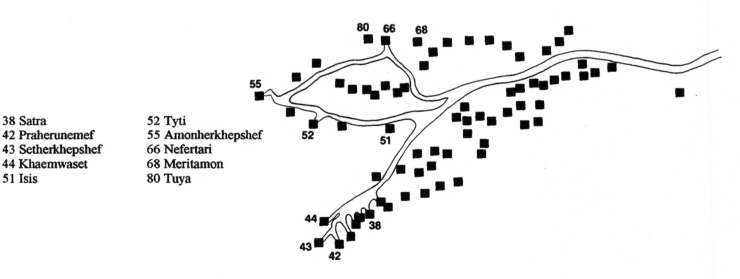

38 Satra
42 Praherunemef
43 Setherkhepshef
44 Khaemwaset
51 Isis

52 Tyti
55 Amonherkhepshef
66 Nefertari
68 Meritamon
80 Tuya

Temple of Hatshepsut at Deir el-Bahri

The temple of Queen Hatshepsut sits in a rocky bay known as Deir el-Bahri and is a magnificent example of the Egyptian ideal of building in harmony with nature. Unlike the temples of a later period, which exhibit the more Greek ideal of man imposing his force upon nature in a controlling way, this lovely temple achieves a blend with the surrounding natural features.

The temple itself tells of the accomplishments of this remarkable queen and is built on three levels.

The first level, on the right side, shows her in the form of a sphinx. This echoed the limestone sphinxes that stood along the edge of the approach to this temple and now reside in New York's Metropolitan Museum. To the left, the first level shows the expedition to Aswan that brought the two great obelisks to the temple of Karnak.

The second level is famous for the Punt expedition reliefs to the south of the causeway ramp and also contains a chapel to the goddess Hathor at the extreme south end. The south wall of the colonnade shows the Queen of Punt with the Egyptian army and the river with shark, squid and turtles. The west or back wall shows a variety of scenes with a rather interesting arrangement. The land of Punt is shown on the south wall and the fleet, seen on the lower register at the corner of the back wall, has the prows pointed towards the south. The returning fleet is shown with their prows toward the north and is seen in the register just above that of the departing fleet. The rest of the west wall shows scenes of the treasures brought back.

From the center and in the upper register moving to the north, is the formal announcement of the success of the expedition before the god Amon. The queen stands at the left with a staff in her hand and faces toward Amon who is enthroned on the right. A long inscription ensues between the queen and the god. Much of this has been very skillfully hacked away, but some is still visible. The titles and encomium (praise) of Hatshepsut and the oracle of Amon have been reproduced below with a translation. This represents only the beginning portion of the entire text that continues onto the north wall and becomes too mutilated for any attempt at a reasonable translation.

The northern side of the terrace colonnade shows Hatshepsut's conception and birth. The god Amon sits with Queen Ahmose (Hatshepsut's mother) upon a bed and offers her the ankh, or life symbol. Khnum is seen forming the baby and her 'ka' on his wheel and finally the queen as child is presented to the other gods.

The area in the extreme northwest corner is dedicated to the god Anubis, the god who presides at the mummification. The intact color here gives an impression of what the whole temple must have been like at the time of original construction.

The third level is not open to the public at the time of this writing, but contains a central court bordered by a colonnade on three sides with a smaller court to the north containing a center altar. The south side of this court holds a series of vaulted rooms that were dedicated to the royal funerary cult with the shrine itself built into the side of the mountain behind.

Translation:

Titulary and Praises of Hatshepsut:

The Horus: Wsrtkaw (Mighty in Ka's); Two Ladies: Fresh in years; Horus of Gold: Divine of Risings; King of Upper and Lower Egypt: Maat-Ka-Re (Hatshepsut), The holy image of Amon, whom he loves, who is upon his throne, whom he has caused to flourish (for her) the inheritance of the Two Lands, the kingship of the South and North, for her he has given that which the sun encompasses and that which Geb and Nut enclose. She has no enemies among the Southerners, she has no opponent among the Northerners; heaven and all countries which the god has created, they work for her in every respect. They come to her with fearful heart, their chiefs with bowed heads, their tribute upon their backs! They present to her their children in quest that they may be given the breath of life because of the great fame of her father Amon, who has placed all lands beneath her sandals.

The Oracle:

The king himself, the King of Upper and Lower Egypt, Maat-Ka-Re (Hatshepsut). The majesty of the court (or palace) petitioned at the throne (steps) of the lord of gods; a command was heard from the great throne, an oracle of the god himself, to search out the paths to Punt, to explore the roads to the myrrh terraces: "I will lead the army upon water and land in order to bring marvels from god's land for this god, the creator of her beauty". It was done according to all which the majesty of this august god commanded, according to the desire of her majesty, so that she may be given life, stability and dominion like Re, forever.

Deir el-Medina: The Workmen's Village

Unique in the history of ancient Egypt is the isolated desert village of the tomb makers of the New Kingdom who worked in the *Great Place* and the *Place of Beauty* as the Valley of the Kings and Queens was known. Today this village is known as Deir el-Medina, but in the time of the scribes Ramose and Sennedjem it was known as *set-ma'at* or the Place of Truth.

From here the workers set off over the two mountain paths, which still exist today, following the rim of the Theban cliffs. They traveled northwest to reach the Great Place and southwest to the Place of Beauty, creating the artistic masterworks in the great royal tombs of the Eighteenth, Nineteenth and Twentieth dynasties. This village was the only permanent residential structure in the whole of the necropolis and the only one sited in the desert away from the cultivation of the Nile valley.

In this village lived some of the finest craftsmen that Egypt had ever known. To visit the village today is to glimpse into the houses of these people who lived there over 3400 years ago, people with special knowledge, craftsmen who made the figures of the gods, caused them to live and knew the secrets of the tomb. It is not surprising then; that some say their voices can still be heard on the wind that sweeps the surrounding cliffs.

Their own tombs, two of which are open to public view, are those of Sennedjem [TT1] whose house is located in the southwest corner of the village and Inherkau [TT359]. They are of a workmanship to rival the royal tombs in either the King's or Queen's valley.

The oldest part of the village was built during the reign of pharaoh Tuthmosis I, but the indication was that his father Amenhotep I had in fact, founded the village. Some two hundred and fifty years later the tradition in place was that this king, now considered a god and patron of the place, was indeed the owner of the village. Four hundred years after his death, the carved figure of Amenhotep I was looked upon in the village as an oracle that "looks into men's hearts" and there are amazing stories of pronouncements by this oracle which settled village disputes.

The village itself is considered to have had a lifespan of some five hundred years by many Egyptologists, but the records of the first two hundred years, from Amenhotep I to the start of the Nineteenth dynasty, are sparse. Much better records appear starting at this time (19th Dynasty) and continuing to the end of the village. The only break in this long span of habitation is in the time of the heretic pharaoh Akhenaten, when the tomb-makers were removed to a new town in Middle Egypt to serve the royalty and nobility at the city of Akhetaten or Tell el-Amarna, as it is known today. They returned to Deir el-Bahri, to their original houses, at the conclusion of this affair. Houses here are clustered together on both sides of a village High Street that runs approximately down the middle, and a wall of unbaked brick surrounds the whole. Within this wall some seventy houses would have been located, all of about the same character; rectangular with four rooms placed one behind the other and a stairway to the roof where the family would retreat to sleep in the hot months of summer.

There would have been a family shrine on one of the walls containing a stela with a carved prayer. Each house appears to have had a central pillar to help support the roof, slots cut in the roof which allowed a small amount of light to enter in, and a wooden door that opened to the main street. The rooms towards the back would have been the kitchen and a storeroom. It is likely that the central street was also roofed so that the whole looked like one large structure from a distance and was entered through one main door on the northern side of the village.

To the north of the village are a group of temples, the main one being dedicated to Hathor and Ma'at. On the south side of the village wall, and running downhill, is the village dump. On the western side up the hill from the village, is the main necropolis, but the surrounding hillsides hold many burials from the village, some indicated by small chapels of unbaked brick or tiny pyramids.

Most of the villages of pharaonic Egypt have not survived to our time. The village of Deir el-Medina affords us an unusual opportunity to step into the front parlors of these ancient people and to unite over a bridge of thousands of years. Take a moment's solitude and walk with them. Listen for their voices as they tell us about their daily lives and concerns. The writings they have left for us in many places along the path tell us that if man fears time, as the saying goes, then surely time fears Egypt!

The Tombs of the Nobles at Sheikh Abd al-Qurna and Asasif

This sacred area, situated at the base of the Theban Hills, is named after the peak of the mountain el-Qurn (the Horn) and the Muslim saint whose tomb site is atop the hill. In practice, the name is applied to the whole area between the fields and the cliffs, but the various groups of houses have individual names. It is a fact that the people of the area at one time lived in the surrounding tombs, the evidence of which will be readily seen by the traveler in the form of smoke damage and debris. These people maintain their homes among the tombs to this day. In past times, it was possible for the tourist to enter any tomb desired. Today however, this is not the case. Many tombs suffered due to this lax policy and now only a few of the tombs remain accessible to the traveler.

Many are difficult to reach but the reward for the persistent visitor more than makes up for the inconvenience. We offer here a selection of the more interesting which are available for public viewing. It is essential that the visitor understand that the tombs are open on a haphazard basis, and on any given day, only certain ones will be available.

The tombs themselves reveal many details about life in ancient times but their main attraction is the hard evidence they supply regarding funerary beliefs. The food and drink that were placed in the tomb were not for the body of the deceased, but rather for that essence which we identify as the ka of the individual and it is the ka which lived in the tomb. The single most important aspect of the tombs here, or the 'focal point' as it is referred to archaeologically, is the false door. This will have written upon it the name of the deceased, his titles in life, and prayers and wishes for the journey to the afterworld. The body itself was usually buried in a subterranean chamber. Often the entrance to this chamber was a shaft that began behind the 'false door' and continued down some number of meters. This is not a hard and fast rule however. This concept of a decorated upper level of rooms and a below ground burial chamber was begun in the Old Kingdom and lasted throughout Pharaonic times.

A number of shapes and sizes are discernible in these tombs but the type most often encountered is the so-called T-shaped tomb. This tomb should have the following elements: (1) a partly rock-cut forecourt with some mud-brick elements and a gate; (2) rock-cut chambers on an upper level with a transverse hall, long passage, an inner room with either a niche to hold statues or rock-cut statues at the rear where a 'false door' may also be located; (3) a subterranean burial chamber and shaft that is sealed after the burial.

Wall subjects would be limited to funerary scenes, scenes having to do with rebirth and scenes of daily life. Here it would be well to remember that hieroglyphs are, in fact, pictures and all pictures have magical qualities attached to them. The wall decorations are meant to live and as such can be beneficial or harmful in nature.

Following is a list of recommended tombs with their numerical designation. A brief description of each is given along with some hieroglyphic translation where possible.

Theban Tomb 1 **(TT1),** the tomb of **Sennedjem** is an artistic masterpiece. The owner is identified by the title "Servant in the Place of Truth." It is in excellent condition and is one of two tombs open in the village of **Deir el-Medina**. One entire wall of the tomb is covered with a view of the Fields of Itaru or the Egyptian Elysian Fields. Water, palm trees, poppies, mandrake and cornflowers are seen, along with our tomb owner and wife as they harvest in the fields. Its beautiful vaulted ceiling and upper parts of the side walls show scenes from the Book of Gates, while the lower registers show pictures of relatives. On the wall opposite the entrance a large scene of Osiris, King of the Dead is seen.

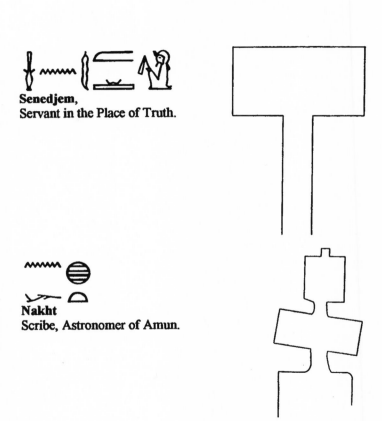

Senedjem,
Servant in the Place of Truth.

The tomb of **Nakht (TT52)** lies a distance away at Qurna. If one follows a steep path about 100 yards north of TT56, the tomb will be reached. Nakht was a scribe and astronomer of Amon during the reign of Tuthmosis IV. Fishing, hunting and harvest scenes from the Nile Delta can be seen to the right of the door. Nakht probably had an estate there. To the left of the door is the funerary banquet scene, perhaps one of the best in Thebes. What is lacking seems to be any depiction of the astronomical duties of the tomb owner.

Nakht
Scribe, Astronomer of Amun.

The tomb of **Ramose (TT55)**, who was the mayor of Thebes and vizier under Akhenaten, shows elements of the Amarna style as his career extended from the reign of Amonhotep III to Amonhotep IV (Akhenaten). The tomb depictions show a transformation in both style and nature as the new religion took hold. The tomb was to have been done in painted relief but this plan was not fully realized. The wall to the left of the entrance shows the funeral procession but the workers were halted before completion; the old king had flown to the sky. Akhenaten was now king and new artistic principals were now laid down. Instead of beginning all over, Ramose decided to continue his tomb with some modifications. Thus we now see the two styles together in one tomb.

Ramose
Mayor of Thebes under Akhenaten

Theban Tomb number 56 **(TT56)**, is the burial place of **Userhet**, a royal scribe whose apparent duty was to cope with the logistics of the army of Amonhotep II. It is found to the south of the tomb of Ramose (TT55 see below) at Sheikh Abd el-Qurna which was, without doubt, the most popular burial place at Thebes. Among the scenes shown are the soldiers lined up for a meal, the barbers coming to shave them and the satisfactory result. Perhaps the most outstanding scene shows the tomb owner in a chariot hunting desert animals and a fox that is caught hanging in a tree.

Userhet
Royal Scribe

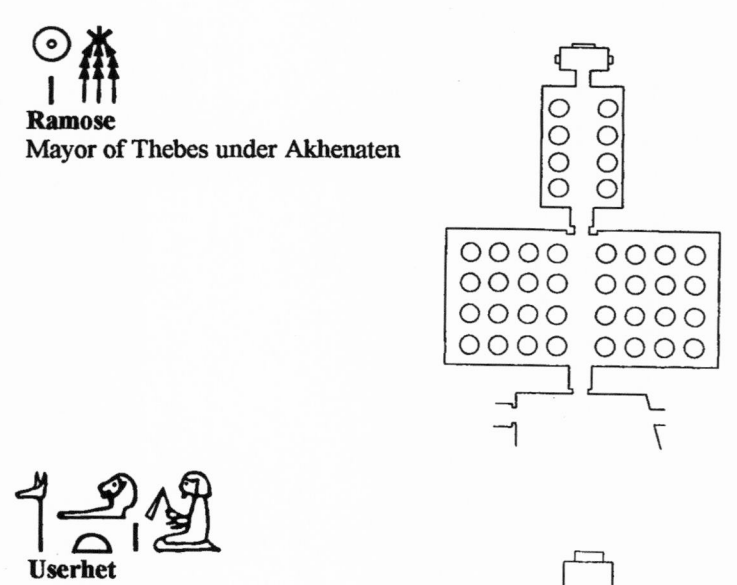

Khaemhet, (TT57) may look unremarkable at first sight, for there is almost no color, but one should look closely at the limestone relief to observe the delicacy and vibrancy of the sculpture. Khaemhet was the overseer of the granaries of Upper and Lower Egypt and this may be the cause of two agricultural activity scenes in his tomb instead of one, as is more usual. The standard scenes of ploughing to harvesting are depicted with some quite unusual detail. Notice the boy taking a break from the labor to play his pipe and the offerings being presented to the god of the harvest. Notice also that field workers are shown wearing sandals when in fact this was not usually the case.

Khaemhet
Royal Scribe; Overseer of the Granaries of Upper and Lower Egypt

The tomb of **Menna (TT69)** continues with the motif of agricultural activities. This is not unusual when one realizes that he was the inspector of estates during the time of Tuthmosis IV. The tomb is in the T-form with the transverse hall containing some very realistic agricultural scenes along with funerary scenes of the owner and his wife before Osiris, which are quite detailed in nature. The artist's fine hand is quite in evidence here along with some very good color. The passage shows fishing, fowling and the bringing of offerings. Also the Abydos pilgrimage is seen here.

Menna
Scribe of the fields of the Lord of the Two Lands of Upper and Lower Egypt

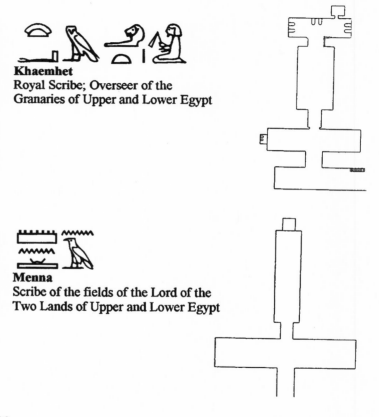

Sennefer (TT96). Sennefer was the mayor of Thebes in the time of Amenhotep II and his tomb is somewhat unusual. The upper chambers of the tomb are closed to the general public but the lower burial chamber, which was not decorated as a rule, but is in this case, can be reached. Here is one of the most spectacular sights in any tomb; a ceiling of grapes and vine leaves for which the uneven surface provides a perfect basis. The color is in a remarkable state of preservation and the wall scenes only serve to enhance the effect. Well worth the effort to reach!

Sennefer
Mayor of Thebes

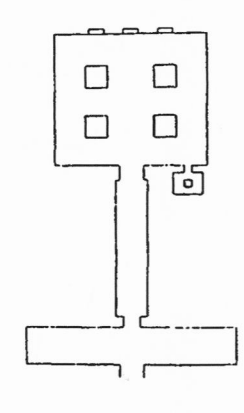

Near the tomb of Sennefer is tomb number 100 (**TT100**) belonging to **Rekhmire** who was the vizier during the reigns of Tuthmosis III and Amenhotep II. The tomb is exceptional, in part due to the height that the ceiling in the passage leading off from the transverse entrance hall attains. This is seen nowhere else in these tombs. There is no explanation as yet for this circumstance. The hall, although somewhat deteriorated, shows us a remarkable procession of tribute bringers and a wonderful array of animals. The passage shows scenes of the workshops in the charge of Rekhmire. The opposite wall holds a banquet depicted in excellent color with funerary rites further towards the interior. These are among the best in the entire Theban necropolis and are a paradigm for all others.

Rekhmire
Governor of Thebes and Visier

The tomb of **Neferronpet, (TT178)** is perhaps one of the best Ramesside period tombs. Located at Khokha, a bit north and west of Qurna, the walls of this tomb are laid out as if in a book. On the left there are fourteen scenes in two registers, which are mainly from the Book of Gates. The right half of the hall shows us the tomb owner, sometimes with his wife, adoring gods in the upper register and the funerary procession in the lower. The inner room again shows the couple before various gods, including the Hathor cow in the mountain, with the lower right scene of Neferronpet inspecting workshops. At the rear are four rock-cut statues against the wall. This makes a very impressive sight as they are painted and in fair condition.

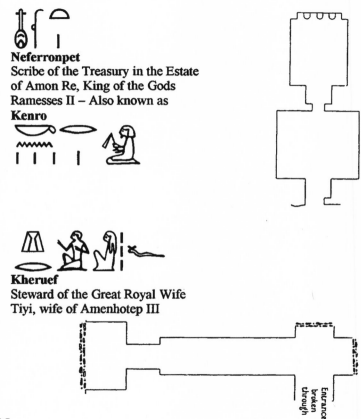

Neferronpet
Scribe of the Treasury in the Estate of Amon Re, King of the Gods
Ramesses II – Also known as
Kenro

Moving to the **Asasif**, north and east, we find the tomb of **Kheruef (TT192),** the steward of Queen Tiyi, wife of Amenhotep III. This tomb, partly ruined, is of great interest. The emphasis here is on the royal family, a motif that will surface in the Amarna period following the death of Amenhotep III. The scenes show the royals in such acts as offering, participating in religious ceremony, and in the festival of erection of the djed pillar which has been at times related to the backbone of the god Osiris. The purpose here is to allow the tomb owner opportunity to show his relationship to the king.

Kheruef
Steward of the Great Royal Wife Tiyi, wife of Amenhotep III

The Colossi of Memnon

In a land where so much seems to hardly notice the passing of time, what was probably the largest of the mortuary temples of Western Thebes leaves hardly a trace for us to see. What is left however, has captured the imagination of people for millennia. These are, of course, the two large seated statues that have become known as the Colossi of Memnon. These two giants sit at what was once the outer entranceway to the mortuary temple of Amonhotep III, the pharaoh who was called "The Magnificent", and ruled over Egypt at the time of its greatest power in the 18th Dynasty.

That nothing survives should perhaps not surprise us as the structure was largely constructed of mud brick and was erected in an area where the annual floodwaters of the Nile could reach it. Time, erosion and the workings of the fellaheen in removing the decayed mud brick for fertilization of the fields have done their work.

These two surviving monuments give mute witness to the grandeur that must have been this mortuary temple. It will be well worth the visitor's time to walk around the site to see it from various points. In this way, one may achieve a feel for the area of the structure. Amonhotep III also built a palace to the south for his Jubilee Festival of the same mud brick material. It too has suffered a similar fate and left us only scant traces.

The statues are made of quartzite and stand about 55ft. in height. They rest upon a base that adds six feet to the total.

The seated pharaoh has his legs flanked by his queen Tiye to the left, and Amenhotep's mother, Mulemula, to the right. Identified by Greek travelers as Memnon, the mythical son of Aurora, the name has stuck over the ages.

The northern statue, which had been severely damaged in an earthquake in the first century BCE, was said to "sing" at dawn. This was undoubtedly due to water collecting in the cracks of the colossus and then evaporating as vapor when the sun hit it in the morning. Confirmation of this is found in the numerous Greek and Latin inscriptions on the base of this one only. Additionally, Pausinia and Juvenal reported the phenomenon in the 2nd century CE. That this is surely the case is confirmed by the fact that it stopped its song in abrupt fashion when Septimius Severus ordered the statue repaired, perhaps to relieve the suffering of old Memnon.

On the south side of the southern statue's throne, one can see the classic scene of the unification of the Two Lands. Here two gods are seen tying a knot in the glyph for windpipe in symbolic unification or the sema-tawy "Binding of the Two Lands". This is done with the use of the heraldic plants of the north and south, the papyrus and the lotus. Above this, the cartouche of the pharaoh can be seen.

The Colossi on Memnon

Medinet Habu: The Temples of Ramesses III

The structure referred to as Medinet Habu is in reality a complex of structures, built at various times and with differing purposes. The oldest part of the complex dates from the 18th Dynasty, built by Queen **Hatshepsut,** completed by **Tuthmosis III,** and is still visible today. The structure is a square-pillared temple that was used during the *Festival of the Valley* as a shrine for the barque of Amon. During this festival the god and his family were removed from their shrines in Karnak and transported across the river to the west bank. Here they moved from one mortuary temple to another in effect visiting their sons, the pharaohs, much as we might visit the graves of deceased relatives today. Only the gates survive of the mud-brick enclosure wall that once surrounded this temple.

The temple was added to over the years by various kings such as **Nectanebo I**, who added a kiosk, and **Taharqa** who added a small pylon. An additional pylon of Ptolemaic date was added later. During the first millennium the belief was that the mound upon which this temple stands was the burial spot of the Ogdoad, the primordial group of eight divinities who were creators of the world with the god Thoth as its lord. The group was composed of four pairs of male and female gods of which the god Amon was one. At the time of a feast known as the *Feast of the Tenth Day* the god Amon of Luxor would travel to Medinet Habu to celebrate rites which would return life to the Ogdoad and so to all creation. The

twenty-fifth and twenty-sixth Dynasties added yet another aspect with the construction of special funerary chapels in the southeast part of the complex for the divine votaresses of Amon. These were members of the royal family who formed this prestigious class of priestesses.

The main part of the complex comprises the temple of **Ramesses III** and is still largely intact with its extremely deep cut hieroglyphs. This structure was dedicated primarily to the worship of the pharaoh and stands at the center of the complex. The main pylon is decorated with the traditional scenes of the king dispatching his enemies, the Asiatics and the Sea Peoples, before Amon-Re on the southern pier and Re-Harakhty on the north side. In a departure from tradition in building, the entrance to the temple shows the form of the so-called *Migdol* or fortified entry. This reflects a military fortress of Asiatic type and is a part of the temple's enclosure wall. Looking up to the right and left while passing through this entrance, the figures of the captives can be seen on the walls.

To the south of the first pylon the remains of the royal palace can be seen. The *Window of Appearances* allowed the king to observe various ceremonies that took place in the temple. This palace served the king from time to time while ceremonies were taking place at the temple and while he was in Thebes, but an additional main purpose was surely one of providing a symbolic residence for the king in the next world.

Importantly however, it provides us with the only example of a royal throne room from the period. On the reverse side of the southern half of the main pylon, a bull-hunting scene can be observed. This artwork is considered by many to be one of the true masterworks of Egyptian art of the Twentieth Dynasty.

Returning to the first court, the king can be seen standing before each pillar of the north portico. Here on the outer northern wall are scenes of the king's battles with the Sea Peoples, which took place in the Delta and were the first great naval battles in history. These battles took place in year eight of the king's reign. Moving into the second court, battle scenes can again be viewed in the southwest corner of the court. Better preserved, however, are the scenes of the *Festival of Min* that was held annually. These scenes can be seen on the western section of the north wall of this court in the upper register. The ithyphallic god can be seen as he was processed along the west bank with long-leaf lettuce being offered to him, which the Egyptians considered an aphrodisiac–quite appropriate for this god!

The main axis then continues through a series of hypostyle halls to the sanctuary with its roof now gone and in a badly damaged state. The king with a group of baboons can be seen on the lintel of the west portico; again showing the solar association of the king as these animals were thought to greet the rising sun every day with their chattering.

The complex had a long history that extended as far as the ninth century CE, with the Coptic town of Djeme on the site. At that time it contained its own church and monastery and was one of the largest sites in the area. It provided intact information regarding the complete history of the complex.

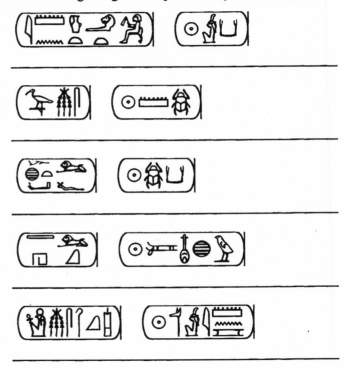

Temple of Horus at Edfu

This temple which stands on the west bank of the Nile at the town of Edfu, is the most complete temple in existence in Egypt. The site itself is most ancient in origin having been used as a sacred venue since predynastic times. The present structure owes its appearance to **Ptolemy III Euergetes** who began to rebuild it in 237 BCE. It was not until 57 BCE. however that the work was completed. A curious aspect of this temple is the number of empty cartouches seen on the walls, perhaps due to the late completion of the temple just prior to the Roman conquest. It may indicate that there was insufficient time to re-dedicate the temple and therefore the kings name was not put into the cartouches. The massive entrance pylon, standing 118ft. shows **Ptolemy XII** conquering his enemies shortly before the roman conquest in 30 BCE.

The temple reliefs are among the best preserved in Egypt. Passing through the pylon, one enters an open court bordered on three sides by columns, and behind these, the wall reliefs that show the festival of the Beautiful Reunion. This festival marked the traveling of the statue of Horus to Dendera, in order to meet that of Hathor, and return by boat to Edfu to celebrate their marriage. Horus of Edfu has associations with the solar deity Re dating from the time of the Pyramid Texts and should not be confused with certain other forms of the deity which appear at a later date.

Beyond this courtyard is the first hypostyle hall, the façade of which depicts both Horus and Hathor and whose gates were opened only at the time of their festival. The reliefs on the interior walls of this hall show the founding of the temple: it's design, the Stretching of the Cord ceremony measuring it's boundaries, digging the first hole and purification of the site. Passing through this gate to the right can be seen the library, the walls carved with titles of the rolls it once held and to the left the robing room where the high priest purified himself and dressed for the rituals.

Moving towards the sanctuary, the second hypostyle hall is passed through. To the left (or west side) is found the so-called Chamber of the Nile, which contained the pure water from the well used by the priests, and the room where perfumes and ointments were prepared. On the right is the opening to the treasury. The offering hall for food offerings is next encountered. Here offerings to the god were placed on altars and this area also gave access to the staircases leading to the roof terrace where the statue of the divinity would be periodically taken to be 're-charged' by the rays of the sun. The reliefs on the walls of these staircases show the priestly procession carrying the statue up to the court of the New Year on one side and then down again on the other.

At the rear of the temple, the sanctuary still contains a polished granite shrine where the cult statue of Horus once stood. If one looks closely, the carvings of the papyrus thicket which represents the primeval mound of creation, where Horus stood on that first day, can still be seen on the inside walls of the shrine. In the side chamber behind the sanctuary a model of the ceremonial boat shrine wherein the cult statue would have been placed for traveling, can be seen. Around this sanctuary runs a corridor, off which are located various chapels used for special rites and storage purposes.

Perhaps the most informative and interesting area of the temple is the outer corridor running around the rear of the temple and closed in by the enclosure wall. These walls contain the story of the struggle between Horus and Seth for the throne of Egypt. These events were performed as part of an annual ceremony known as the Triumph of Horus. The ritual of the Ten Harpoons which ended with the killing of Seth in the form of a hippopotamus and Horus sailing in victory on the sacred lake, were the two main elements of this festival. The inscriptions here give the whole story of the battle between these gods and are one of the few theological accounts to survive to our time

The Temple of Horus at Edfu was begun by Ptolemy III and completed 180 years later. Except for Karnak, it is the largest and best preserved in Egypt

Ptolemy III (Euergetes I) 246-222

Ptolemy XII (Neos Dionysos) 80-58, 55-51

Temple of Kom Ombo, Dedicated to Two Gods

Situated on the ancient site of Ombos, a place occupied from prehistoric times, this temple is unique in its dedication to two gods. The temple is one of singular design, with a double row of doors and two parallel processional routes leading to a double sanctuary. The northern section is dedicated to Horus the Elder or Harwer, and the southern section is dedicated to the crocodile-god, Sobek.

The general layout is one of Ptolemaic style as the temple was originally built around 150 BCE and added to by several Roman emperors from Augustus and Tiberius Caesar to Macrinus about 217 CE. Foundations are all that remain of the pylon, which represented the king entering the temple. Beyond this, to the inside of the court, the king is again shown, this time leaving his palace with standards in his escort. The court itself is paved with a columned portico and an altar. Approaching the sanctuary, reliefs show the king in the act of purification in the facade of the pronaos.

Once in the pronaos, the columns repeat the idea of the dual nature of this temple showing papyrus capitals on the northern side and lotus ones on the south. The ceiling is decorated with astronomical images while the walls show the king being purified and the consecration of the temple. Of further interest is the west wall of the hypostyle hall, which shows an inventory of sacred places in Egypt, the gods of the main towns, and local as well as national festivals. This is located between the two doors of the central axis. The following room shows a depiction of the goddess Seshat in the act of *stretching the cord*. She is identified by the inverted horns and star-like device on a standard atop her head.

Moving into the offering hall a lion goddess can be seen. She was there in order to oversee the offerings made on each day of the year and was assisted by bull or ram-headed gods. To the north of the last room, the Court of the New Year would be found, but it, unfortunately, no longer exists. However, of singular interest, is part of the ceiling of the Pure Place that still can be seen. This Pure Place is where the statue of the god was dressed for the Festival of the New Year, and the ceiling was decorated with two images of the sky goddess Nut. The relief shows on the body of the larger image, winged solar discs and on the smaller the different phases of the moon, as a barque of the night sails between the two.

Some of the most interesting reliefs are to be seen on the outer wall at the rear of the temple. On the left, at eye level, are two goddesses seated upon birth stools. Behind them, laid out upon a table, is what appears to be a selection of surgical instruments. We leave the identification of their various usages to the imagination of the traveler.

On the opposite wall, along the centerline of the temple, a small inset stone with carvings of a pair of eyes and ears on either side. Here is the place where the local people could come to petition the god. This is as close to the sanctuary as the common person was allowed. Interesting to note is that, behind this stone and hidden in a chamber in the wall, a priest would place himself and respond to the questions asked of the divinity. The eyes and ears of the god were a constant reminder that he could see and hear all, and whom the people, no doubt, believed they were addressing. Behind the wall and inside the temple, the entrance to this secret chamber can still be found in an open shaft between the floor of the two sanctuaries.

To the south of the temple, a chapel that was dedicated to the goddess Hathor by Domitian, contains crocodile mummies. These are from a nearby crocodile necropolis to the southeast.

The picture at the right is a portion of the ceiling from the Pure Place where the statue of the god was dressed during the Festival of the New Year. The double image of the sky goddess shows the larger image with a winged sun disk passing through her body while she swallows the disk of the sun at the lower right. The lower image shows the moon passing through her body. Once every twenty-eight days the moon was thought to enter the underworld and join the sun in its rejuvenation.

Between the two images, the goddess Nephthys holds the barque of night with an image of the nocturnal sun god transformed into a child at the front of the vessel. It was the task of Isis and Nephthys to keep the barque in motion between them. Cosmographical texts related to other scenes of this nature speak of the totality of the course of the sun god indicating the cosmic realms related to his journeys; the primeval waters (Nun), the Netherworld (Duat), and the sky (Nut).

The Temple of Isis at Philae

The temples of Isis and Harpocrates (Horus the Younger) were moved to their present position on the island of Agilkia from Philae to escape the rising waters of the High Dam, which would have completely covered it. Originally the temple was erected between the 26th dynasty and the Roman period. Nectanebo built the portico, which is at the top of the entry stairway, in the 30th dynasty. The forecourt is the next encountered, and is flanked by two colonnades.

Immediately behind the eastern colonnade stands the temple of Aresnuphis, a Graeco-Roman god who has an association with Isis. A temple follows it to Mandulis, the Nubian Horus. These are at a right angle to the colonnade. Close by the front of the main temple to the east, and again at a right angle to it, is a temple to **Imhotep**, the builder of the Step Pyramid. By Graeco-Roman times he had become venerated as a healer and a holy man.

The main pylon shows **Ptolemy XII** offering to Isis, Horus and Hathor. At a right angle and in front of the east pylon **Ptolemy II** had build a gateway. This may have been the original approach to the temple. Past this first pylon, the central court opens to the east into a series of rooms and to the west, the mamissi or birth-room. This consists of a pronaos and three following rooms which were built by **Ptolemy VI**. Here the birth of Horus was celebrated.

The second pylon is at a slight angle to the east and follows the main route of the temple. This opens to a pronaos where the vulture appears on the ceiling. The barques of the day and night can be seen to the sides. The sanctuary proper consists of a series of rooms that form an independent unit where the granite naos still exists.

Returning to the second pylon, a right turn (west) will lead you to Hadrian's Gateway and what was considered to be the source of the Nile. Here a staircase leads to a passage down to the river upon whose walls are carved some most interesting scenes. Starting on the left near the river a crocodile carrying the mummy of Osiris to the island of Biggeh is seen. Above is the resurrected Osiris with Horus beneath the sky. To the right is the Nile god, Hapy, who is hidden in a cave on Biggeh Island. A vulture and a falcon are seen above a grotto where Hapy is shown with a magic serpent pouring water from vases at the Nile's source. To the right of this is a crudely carved figure of a man and a badly written inscription alongside. This is one of the last recorded inscriptions ever written in hieroglyphs from 394 CE. North of this is a temple to Harpocrates (Horus the Younger) and to the south is a Nilometer.

On the east side of the island is a small Temple of Hathor. **Ptolemy VI** and **VIII** dedicated the columns of this temple to the goddess. These have scenes of musicians and the dwarf god Bes dancing and playing a small drum, and of a rather strange ape figure playing a flute. These antics were designed to appease the gods, in all probability.

To the south lies the Kiosk of Trajan, which is also known as Pharaoh's Bed.

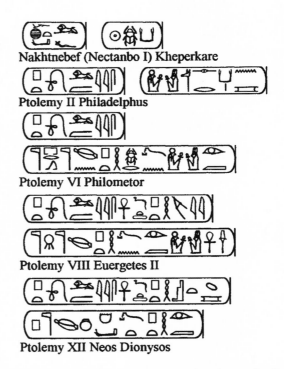

Nakhtnebef (Nectanbo I) Kheperkare

Ptolemy II Philadelphus

Ptolemy VI Philometor

Ptolemy VIII Euergetes II

Ptolemy XII Neos Dionysos

Right to left. Isis, Horus, and Hathor are carved into the first pylon at Philae. A defaced lion still guards the entrance. This pylon was constructed during the time of Ptolemy XII Neos Dionysos, 1ˢᵗ c. CE.

95

The private tombs at Qubbet el-Hawa.
Inset: The tomb of Sarenput II

Aswan: The Tombs of Qubbet el-Hawa

96

The area of Aswan, or Elephantine as it was called in ancient times, is considered the gateway to Nubia. The locale takes it's name from the rock formations in the from of elephants which can be seen from the Nile while crossing the river on the sides of the islands. Here is located the unfinished obelisk and the fantastic temple of Philae, which can only be reached by boat.

High above the Nile, on the west side of the river at Aswan, lay the tombs of Qubbet el-Hawa, the "Caves of the Wind". This site is not to be missed, as the Nile view from the cliff trail, in both directions, is incomparable. Here are the tombs of the nobles from the late Old Kingdom to the Middle Kingdom. One can not fail to notice the site as it is illuminated after dark, and during the day the coffin slides, ramps which lead from the tomb entrance cliffs down to the river, are the most distinguishing landmark on the far western bank.

The climb is difficult, but camels and donkeys are always available for hire at the ticket house and will carry one in relative comfort to the first tomb, that of **Sarenput I.**

The tomb of the Sarenput I is fronted by six pillars in an open courtyard with an outer wall showing scenes of the owner hunting with his dogs and family and being entertained by singers. The tomb is cut back into the rock of the cliff. The character of the stone is worth a mention as it is colored with the minerals in the rock. At the back is an offering place and little else survives.

The tomb of one **Hekaib** can be seen along the path. The tomb shows a doubled columned facade and interesting wall reliefs. These show hunting and fishing scenes along with a bullfight. Hekaib had a reputation as a wise man and became deified in later times.

Moving south down the rocky path that runs in front of the tombs, the tomb of **Harkhuf** is encountered. This Sixth Dynasty official traveled to Africa and returned with a dwarf (probably a pygmy), during the regin of Pepy II. The long autobiographical text in front of the tomb includes a letter sent to him by this king telling him to take the utmost in care to assure the safe return of the pygmy for the young king. You can see the hieroglyph of this dancing pygmy approximately in the middle of the text.

Farther on down the path and in line with the coffin slides sits the tomb of **Sarenput II.** It is worth the walk to see this tomb as it contains an unusual passage exhibiting life size mummiform statues of the owner. The paint on these is still in excellent condition and an offering scene in the back of the tomb also shows remarkable color. The offerings are dedicated to the local god and goddess of Aswan, Khnum, Lord of the Cool Water at Elephantine and Satis, Lady of Elephantine.

Abu Simbel: The Temples of Ramesses II and Nefertari

The two temples which today stand atop a portion of the Libyan mountains and overlook the Nile (Lake Nasser), were moved from their position at the base of these cliffs 210 ft. below, to save them from the rising Nile waters behind the High Dam. All who view this can not help but feel that this was a feat of engineering that the ancient Egyptians themselves would have marveled at. This was accomplished in 1968 with the aid of a multi-national force and UNESCO. Had this not been done, these magnificent temples would have been lost to the world.

The main temple is the one situated to the south of the site. Four colossal seated statues of Ramesses II greet the visitors as they wind their way around the base to the main

entrance. Each of these stands 65 ft. in height with the top of the temple reaching a height of 108 ft. The king, a benevolent smile upon his face, sits upon his throne with the double crown of Egypt upon his head. At his feet are the statues of queen Nefertari, princesses, and the queen mother.

The sides of the thrones show representations of conquered nations either to the north or south of the entranceway, depending upon their geographical location. Atop the temple facade stand 22 baboons with arms up-lifted to greet the rising sun with the god Re directly above the entrance.

The temple extends 180 ft. into the rock with two columned halls preceding the sanctuary. The first contains square-cut pillars cut from the rock and show Osiriform figures of the king in front of them. The walls are covered with scenes of Ramesses II's military victories including the famous battle of Kadesh with the Hittites on the Orontes river in Syria. That this battle was at best a draw for the Egyptians would not be easily discernible from the story told here! On the left, Ramesses is shown charging a fortress on a chariot and to the right is a series of scenes showing the Egyptian camp, captured Hittite spies, the battle and piles of severed hands used to count the dead being inspected by the king. Off this hall are a number of small side chambers used for temple storage purposes. These show the king before the various gods of Egypt.

The second hall shows Ramesses with the gods and then leads to the sanctuary where the king is seen seated with three other gods; (from the right) Re-Harakhti (red), Ramesses II (red), Amon-Re (blue) and Ptah (white). These divine guardians of Egypt's three major cities (Heliopolis, Thebes and Memphis) surround the deified king. Twice a year, on October 20 and February 20, the time of the solstices, the rays of the morning sun shine straight into the temple and illuminate the seated statues at the rear. This has the power of reinvigorating the figures with new life and divine energy. The reconstructed temple was aligned so that this still occurs.

The north temple at Abu Simbel is considered unique among Egyptian temples because this temple is dedicated to a queen, Queen Nefertari, wife of Ramesses II. More unusual is that the statues of Queen Nefertari are depicted as equal in size to those of the king. There is only one other parallel to this in ancient Egyptian architecture, that of Amonhotep III for his queen, Tiy, at Sedeinga; a Nubian site between the Second and Third Cataracts of the Nile.

Throughout this temple the queen appears as often as her husband and it is only at the very end, on the rear wall, that Ramesses takes precedence in offering to Hathor who emerges to protect him. In the first hall Hathor pillars replace the Osiriform pillars of the Ramesses Temple, and the hall is decorated with reliefs showing Ramesses dispatching various enemies in the queen's presence while she offers to Mut and Hathor on the far wall. Farther inside, in the sanctuary, the goddess Hathor appears as the Hathor cow, emerging from the cavern in the mountain, the domain of Hathor, and protecting the breastplate of Ramesses II. To the south, the wall shows Ramesses doing glorifications and to the north is Nefertari doing divine rites of worship.

Some scholars believe that the dedication of this temple was the last official act of this great queen whose name means "The One to whom Beauty Pertains" and who carries the epithet "for whom the sun shines." Indications are that one of her daughters, most likely Meryetamon her eldest, stood in for her at the ceremonies while she remained on her barque, too weak to participate. In any event, this is the last we hear of this beloved queen of Ramesses II to whom he raised this temple, the only one of it's kind in Egypt!

On the following page is a translation of the glyphic inscriptions appearing on the facade of the Northern Temple at Abu Simbel including the framing text and the texts on the six buttresses.

Inscriptions at the Temple of Hathor Dedicated to Nefertari, Abu Simbel North Temple

Uppermost across the top of the temple read:

Left (South)
Live the Good God who tramples down the Nubians, King of Upper and Lower Egypt, Usermaatre-Setepenre, given life forever!

Right (North)
Live the Good God, Image of Re, mighty of sword, whose like has never been, King of Upper and Lower Egypt, Usermaatre-Setepenre, Son of Re, Ramesses (II), Beloved of Amon.

Panel over the doorway, two vertical columns to the left, read left to right.
(1) *Beloved of the Ruler of the Two Lands, (2) The Good God, Lord of the Two Lands, Usermaatre-Setepenre.*

Over doorway, two vertical columns to the right, read right to left.
(1) *Beloved of "Re of Rulers", (2) the Son of Re, Lord of Risings, Ramesses (II), Beloved of Amon.*

Over first statue south of doorway
Ruler of the two lands, beloved of Amon.

Buttress to the left of first statue.
King of Upper and Lower Egypt, Usermaatre-Setepenre, Son of Re, Ramesses (II) Beloved of Amon, beloved of the Ruler of the Two Lands, given life like Re forever.

Next buttress south (left).
A Temple of great and mighty monuments for the Great Royal Wife Nefertari, Beloved of Mut, for whose sake the sun does shine, given life and beloved;

Last southern buttress.
Made by the King of Upper and Lower Egypt, Lord of the Two Lands, Usermaatre-Setepenre, Son of Re, of his body, Ramesses (II), Beloved of Amon, beloved of Amon like Re, forever and ever.

Over first statue north of doorway.
Re of Rulers, beloved of Atum.

Buttress to the right of first statue.
King of Upper and Lower Egypt, Usermaatre-Setepenre; he has made a Temple by excavation in the mountain, of eternal workmanship in Nubia,

Next buttress north (right).
(which) the King of Upper and Lower Egypt, Usermaatre-Setepenre, has made (for) the Great Royal Wife, Nefertari, Beloved of Mut, in Nubia, like Re forever and ever.

Last northern buttress.
His Majesty commanded to be made a Temple in Nubia by excavation in the mountain; never has the like been done before, except (in this instance) for the "Beloved of Amon."

Appendix

Translations of the Examples

Translation of Hatshepsut's Obelisk at Karnak

West Face

The Horus, Mighty or Powerful of Kas; Two Ladies; Fresh (or Flourishing) in Years; Horus of Gold; Divine of Risings (or Diadems; crowns or insignia) *(for a discussion of this and example see Gardiner pg. 72 or S. Quirke 'Who Were the Pharaohs?' pg 15-18 for discussion of 'Risings in this sense with O.K. antecedents esp. in P. Westcar)*; Lord of the Two Lands; Maat-ka-re; She made (it) as her monument for her father Amon, lord of the Thrones of the Two Lands *(see Gardiner pg. 575)*, erecting for him two great obelisks at the august gate: "Amon is Great in Terror," with very much electrum that illuminates the Two Lands like the sun; never was *(Gardiner pg. 377)* the like made since the beginning. May the Son of Re, Khnm(t)-Amon, Hatshepsut, perform given life *(Gardiner pg. 368)* for him, like Re, forever.

South Face

The Horus; Mighty or Powerful of Kas; The King of Upper and Lower Egypt; Maat-ka-re, the glorious image of Amon, who he has caused *(Gardiner pg. 275)* to appear as king upon the throne of Horus in the face of *(Gardiner pg. 133)* the splendors *(see 'Punt reliefs' Breasted v.II pg.120)* of the Great House, who the great ennead of gods have brought up *(Gardiner pg. 304-7)* to be *(Gardiner pg.65)* mistress of the circuit of the sun; They have united her with life, satisfaction and joy in front of the living; Son of Re, Khnm(t)-Amon, Hatshepsut, beloved *(Gardiner pg. 278-9)* of Amon-Re, king of the gods, given life like Re, forever.

North Face

Same as west as far as Maat-ka-re.

Her father Amon has established (caused to establish) her great name Maat-ka-re upon the august Ished tree; moreover, her annals are millions of years united with life, stability and dominion; Son of Re, Khnm(t)-Amon, Hatshepsut, beloved of Amon-Re, King of the gods, heir to this beautiful, stone carved monument (when) she celebrated for him the first occurrence of the Heb-sed festival, (so that) she may do, given life forever.

East Face

Same as south as far as Maat-ka-re.

Beloved of Amon-Re; Her majesty made the name of her father established upon this monument, enduring, when favor was given to the King of Upper and Lower Egypt, Lord of the Two Lands, Aakheperkare (Tuthmosis I), by the majesty of this august god, when the two great obelisks were erected by her majesty on the first occasion (of jubilee), the lord of the gods said: Indeed, your father, King of Upper and Lower Egypt, Aakheperkare gave command (placed under the foot?) to erect obelisks and your majesty will repeat *(Gardiner pg. 253)* the monuments, (so that) you may do *Gardiner pg. 395)* "may she live!" *(Gardiner pg. 239)* forever.

Note: Hatshepsut built obelisks as her father had done. The "favor" referred to is in the fact of the oracle of Amon coming to the queen in regards to her father. This was a favor shown to her father.

Dynastic Chronology with the Names of Rulers

Dates are approximate. The margin of error may be as much as one or two centuries for the earliest periods and 50 years for the later Dynasties. From the Macedonian Dynasty onward, dates are exact within one year. The reign of the kings listed in the First and Second Intermediate Periods (which were times of chaos) lasted a very short time, perhaps as little as one-day. * Indicates those rulers represented on the Abydos King Table.

Predynastic Period (Upper Egyptian Sequence)

Badarian Culture	c. 5000-4500
Naqada I (Amratian) Culture	c. 4500-3700
Naqada II (Gerzean) Culture	c. 3700-3200
Naqada III *Dynasty '0'*	c. 3200-3050
Scorpion	
Narmer	

Proto-Dynastic Period   c. 3050-2686

First dynasty   c. 3050-2813
- *Hor-Aha/Meni
- *Teti
- *Djer
- *Djety
- *Den
- *Anedjid
- *Semerkhet
- *Qa'a

Second Dynasty   c. 2813-2686
- *Hetepsekhemwy
- *Nebre (also Reneb)
- *Ninetjer
- *Weneg
- *Sened
- *Sekhemib/ Peribsen
- *Neferkasokar
- *Khasekhemwy

Old Kingdom   c. 2686-2180

Third Dynasty   c. 2686-2613

*Nebka (Horus Sanakht)	2686-2668
*Djoser (Horus Netjerykhet)	2686-2668
*Djoserteti (Horus Sekhemkhet)	2649-2643
*Horus Khaba	2643-2637
*Huni (Horus Qahedjet)	2637-2613

Fourth Dynasty   c. 2613-2498

*Sneferu	2613-2589
*Khufu	2589-2566
*Djedefre	2566-2558
*Khafre	2558-2532
*Menkaura	2532-2504

Nebka (?)
*Shepseskaf   2504-2500

*Djedkara
*Neferkara IV
*Merenhor
*Neferkamin I, Seneferk
*Nikare
*Neferkare V
*Neferkahor
*Neferkare VI
*Neferkamin II
*Qakare
*Neferkaure
*Neferkauhor
*Neferirkare II

Fifth Dynasty   *c. 2498-2345*
*Userkaf   2498-2491
*Sahure   2491-2477
*Neferirkare   2477-2467
Shepseskare-Ini   2467-2460
*Neferefre   2460-2453
*Niuserre-Izi   2453-2422
*Menkauhor   2422-2414
*Djedkare-Isesi   2414-2375
*Unas   2375-2345

Sixth Dynasty   *c. 2345-2181*
*Teti   2345-2333
*Userkare   ?
*Pepi I Merire   2332-2283
*Merenre   2283-2278
*Pepi II Neferkare   2278-2181
*Nemtiemsaef   ?

Ninth and Tenth Dynasties   *c. 2160-2040*
Meryibre
Neferkara
Wahkare
Neferkare
Mery.....
Nebkare
Merykare

First Intermediate Period   c. 2180-2060

Seventh and Eighth Dynasties   *c. 2180-2160*
*Netjerkara
*Menkara
*Neferkara II
*Neferkara III

Eleventh Dynasty   *c. 2160-2066*
Mentuhotep I
Intef I
Intef II
Intef III

Middle Kingdom (Thebes)   c. 2066-1650

Eleventh Dynasty   *c. 2066-1991*

*Mentuhotep II	2066-2014
*Mentuhotep III	2014-2001
Mentuhotep IV	2001-1991

Twelfth Dynasty (Theban)   *c. 1991-1782*

*Amenemhat I	1991-1962
*Senwosret I	1971-1926
*Amenemhat II	1929-1865
*Senwosret II	1897-1878
*Senwosret III	1878-1841
*Amenemhat III	1842-1797
*Amenemhet IV	1798-1786
Queen Sobeknefru	1785-1782

Thirteenth Dynasty   *c. 1781-1650*

Khusekhemre/Wegaf
Sekhemkare
Sekhemre-khutowi
Sekhemkare
Sehetepibre
Sankhibre
Smenkare
Tetepibre
Swadjkare
Nedjemibre

Khaankhre
Auibre-Hor
Sedjefkare
Sekhemre-khutawi (Sobekhotep II)
Userkare
Smenkhkare
Sehotepkare (Intef IV)
Sobekhotep III
Khasekhemre/Neferhotep I
Khaneferre/Sobekhotep IV
Khaneferre/Sobekhotep V
Wahibre
Merneferre/Ay
Merhetepre/Sobekhotep VI
Mersekhemre/Neferhotep II
Merkaure/Sobekhotep VII
Djedneferre
Swahenre

Fourtenth Dynasty

Nehesy (Eastern delta)

Second Intermediate Period c. 1782-1570

Fifteenth Dynasty (Hyskos)   *c. 1663-1555*

Sheshi
Yakubher
Khyan
Apepi I

Apepi II	
Sixteenth Dynasty	*c. 1663-1555*
Anather	
Yakobaan	
Seventeenth Dynasty (Thebes)	*c. 1663-1570*
Sobekemsaf II	
Intef VII (Nubkheperre)	
Tao I	c. 1633
Tao II	c. 1574
Kamose (Wadjkheperru)	c. 1573-1570

New Kingdom   1570-1075

Eighteenth Dynasty	*1570-1291*
*Ahmos I	1570-1546
*Amenhotep I	1551-1524
Tuthmoside Period	
*Tuthmosis I	1524-1518
*Tuthmosis II	1518-1508
*Tuthmosis III	1504-1450
Queen Hatshepsut (Maatkare)	1498-1483
*Amenhotep II	1453-1419
*Tuthmosis IV	1419-1386
*Amenhotep III	1386-1349
Amarna Period	
Amenhotep IV/Akhenaten	1350-1334
Semenkhkare	1336-1334

Tutankhamon	1334-1325
Ay	1325-1321
*Horemheb	1321-1293
Ramesside Period	
Ninteenth Dynasty	*1293-1185*
*Ramesses I	1293-1291
*Seti I	1291-1278
Ramesses II	1279-1212
Merenptah	1212-1202
Amenmesses	1202-1199
Seti II	1199-1193
Siptah	1193-1187
Queen Tausert	1187-1185
Twentieth Dynasty	*1185-1070*
Setnakhte	1185-1182
Ramesses III	1182-1151
Ramesses IV	1151-1147
Ramesses V	1145-1141
Ramesses VI	1141-1133
Ramesses VII	1133-1128
Ramesses VIII	c. 1127
Ramesses IX	1126-1108
Ramesses X	1108-1098
Ramesses XI	1098-1070

Third Intermediate Period 1069-525

The High Priests (at Thebes) 1080-945

Herihor	1080-1074
Piankh	1074-1070
Pinedjem I	1070-1032
Masaherta	1054-1046
Menkheperre	1045-992
Smendes II	992-990
Pinedjem II	990-969
Psusennes	969-945

Twenty-first Dynasty (at Tanis) 1069-945

Smendes I	1069-1043
Amenemnisu	1043-1039
Psusennes I	1039-991
Amenemope	993-984
Osorkon the Elder	984-978
Siamun	978-959
Psusennes II	959-945

Twenty-second Dynasty (at Tanis) 945-712

Sheshonq I	945-924
Osorkon I	924-889
Sheshonq II	c. 890
Takelot I	889-874
Osorkon II	874-850
Takelot II	850-825

Sheshonq III	825-773
Pami	773-767
Sheshonk V	767-730
Osorkon IV	730-715
Harsiese (at Thebes)	870-860

Twenty-third Dynasty (Libyan) 818-712

Pedibastet	818-793
Sheshonq IV	793-787
Osorkon III	787-759
Takelot III	764-757
Rudamon	757-754
Iuput	754-715
Peftjauabastet (at Herakleopolis)	
Nimlot (at Hermopolis)	

Twenty-fourth Dynasty (at Sais) 727-715

Tefnakht	727-720
Bakenrenef	720-715

Twenty-fifth (Kushite) Dynasty c. 747-656

Piankhi (Piyi)	747-716
Shabaka	716-702
Shebitku	702-690
Taharqa	690-664
Tanutamun	664-656

Late Period   **664-332**

Twenty-sixth (Saite) Dynasty   *664-525*
    Psamtik I   664-610
    Nekau   610-595
    Psamtik II   595-589
    Wahibre   589-570
    Ahmos II   570-526
    Psamtik III   526-525

Twenty-seventh Dynasty (Persian-1) 525-404
    Cambyses II   525-522
    Darius I   521-486
    Xerxes   485-465
    Artaxerxes I   465-424
    Darius II   423-405
    Artaxerxes II   405-359

Twenty-eighth Dynasty   *404-399*
    Amyrtaeus   403-399

Twenty-ninth Dynasty   *399-380*
    Nefaarud I   399-393
    Hakor   393-380

Thirtyeth Dynasty   *380-343*
    Nakhtnebef (Nectanbo I)   380-362
    Djedhor   362-360
    Nakhtnebef (Nectanbo II)   360-343

Thirty-first Dynasty (Persian-2) 343-332
    Artaxerxes III   343-338
    Arses   338-336
    Darius III   336-332

Greek Period   **332-30 BCE**

Macedonian Dynasty   *332-305 BCE.*
    Alexander the Great   332-323
    Philip Arrhidaeus   323-317
    Alexander IV   317-305

Ptolemaic Dynasty   *305-30 BCE*
    Ptolemy I Soter   305-282
    Ptolemy II Philadelphus   285-246
    Ptolemy III Euergetes   246-222
    Ptolemy IV Philopator   222-205
    Ptolemy V Epiphanes   205-180
    Ptolemy VI Philometor   180-164, 163-145
    Ptolemy VII Neos Philopater   145
    Ptolemy VIII Euergetes II   170-163,145-116
    Ptolemy IX Soter II   116-110, 109-107, 88-80
    Ptolemy X Alexander I   110-109, 107-88
    Ptolemy XI Alexander II   80
    Ptolemy XII Neos Dionysos   80-58, 55-51
    Queen Berenice IV   58-55
    Cleopatra VII   51-30
    Ptolemy XV Caesarion   36-30

Selected Bibliography

Bell, Lanny — "Luxor Temple and Cult of Royal Ka." Journal of Near Eastern Studies (JNES) 44 (1985):251-94.

Betz, Hans D., ed. — The Greek Magical Papyri in Translation. Chicago: University of Chicago Press, 1986.

Borghouts, Joris F. — Ancient Egyptian Magical Texts. Religious Texts Translation Series, NISABA, Leiden: E.J. Brill, 1978. "The Magical Texts of Papyrus Leiden 1 348. " Oudheidkundig Mededelingen Rijksmuseum Oudheden (OMRO) vol 51. Leiden: E.J. Brill, 1971.

Breasted, Jmnes H. — Ancient Records of Egypt. Chicago, 1906.

Budge, E.A. Wallis — The Book of the Dead. Facsimiles of the Papyri of Hunefer, Anhai, Kerasher, and Netchmet with Supplementary Text from the Papyrus of Nu. London: British Museum, 1899. Egyptian Magic. London: Kegan Paul, 1901 (reprinted NY Dover, 1971).

Campbell, J. — The Masks of God. Ptimitive Mythology. Penguin 1991.

Dunham, D, & Simpson, W.K. — The Mastaba of Queen Mersyankh 111. MFA, Boston, 1974.

Faulkner, R.O. — A Concise Dictionary of Middle Egyptian. Griffith Institute, Oxford, 1981. Ancient Egyptian Pyramid Texts. Warininster: Aris & Phillips, Ltd., 1969. Ancient Egyptian Coffin Texts, vols. 1-3. Wanninster: Aris & Phillips, Ltd., 1973. The Egyptian Book of the Dead. Chronicle Books, San Francisco, 1994.

Gardiner, Sir Alan H. — Egyptian Grammar, 3rd ed. London, Oxford University Press: 1973.

Grimal, Nicolas — A History of Ancient Egypt. Blackwell Publishers, Inc. Cambridge, 1996.

Hart, G. — Egyptian Myths. University of Texas Press, Austin, 1995.

Hobson, Christine — The World of the Pharaohs. Thames and Hudson, New York, 1987.

Hornung, Erich — Conceptions of God in Ancient Egypt - The One and the Many. (English translation). Cornell: Cornell University Press, 1982. The Ancient Egyptian Books of the Afterlife. Comell, 1999.

Jacq, Christian	Egyptian Magic. (English translation). Wiltshire: Aris & Phillips, 1985.
James, T.G.H.	Pharaoh's People: Scenes from Life in Imperial Egypt. The University of Chicago Press, 1984.
Knopf, A.A. ed.	Egypt. New York, 1995.
Lehner, Mark	The Complete Pyramids. Thames and Hudson, New York, 1997.
Lesko, Leonard	The Ancient Egyptian Book of Two Ways. Berkeley: University of California Press, 1972.
Lichtheim, Miriam	Ancient Egyptian Literature, vol. L Berkeley: University of California Press, 1973. Ancient Egyptian Literature, vol. 11. Berkeley: University of California Press, 1976. Ancient Egyptian Literature, vol. 111. Berkeley: University of California Press, 1980.
Manniche, Lise	City of the Dead,- Thebes in Egypt. 1987. British Museum Publications, London, 1987.
McDonald, John K.	House of Eternity; The Tomb of Nefertari. J. Paul Getty Trust, Los Angeles, 1996.
Porter, B. & Moss, R.	Topographical Bibliography of Ancient Egyptian Hieroglyphic Texts, Reliefs, and Paintings. Vol 1, 11, 111. Oxford, Oxford University Press, 1927.
Qurike, Stephen	Who Were the Pharaohs? Dover Publications, Inc. Mineola, N.Y. 1996.
Redford, Donald B.	Pharaonic King-Lists, Annals and Day-Books. Mississauga, 1986.
Reeves, N & Wilkinson, R.	The Complete Valley of the Kings. Thames and Hudson, New York, 1996.
Romer, John	Ancient Lives. Holt, Rinehart and Winston, New York, 1984.
Schafer, Byron E., ed	Religion in Ancient Egypt -- Gods, Myths and Personal Practice. Ithaca: Comell University Press, 1991.
Siliotti, Alberto	Egypt,- The Splendors of an Ancient Civilization. Thames and Hudson, New York, 1998.
Simpson, W.K.	The Mastabas of Qar and Idu. Vol 11, MFA, Boston, 1976.
Wilkinson, Richard H.	Reading Egyptian Art. Thames and Hudson, 1992. Symbol and Magic in Egyptian Art. London: Thames & Hudson, 1994.

About the Authors

The authors, Thomas F. Mudloff and Ronald E. Fellows examine the serdab at the Step Pyramid in Saqqara while King Djoser watches through peepholes. The serdab is tilted up 13° toward the northern sky where the king joined the circumpolar stars, his brethren. The original statue is in the Cairo Museum, but an excellent replica remains in the serdab to welcome visitors.

Egyptologist Thomas F. Mudloff, left, teaches courses in archaeology and anthropology at Northwestern University (University College) and in Egyptology at the Field Museum of Natural History in Chicago. He frequently lectures on a wide range of subjects including ancient Egyptian religion, myth, magic and language. He has excavated in the Near East and has conducted tours of Egypt, Syria and Jordan since 1984. A member of the International Association of Egyptologists, he often consults with museum curators on the translation of ancient Egyptian writing in their exhibits.

Ronald E. Fellows is an author and publisher, and editor of 𝕿𝖍𝖊 𝕲𝖑𝖞𝖕𝖍 magazine, the journal of the Archaeological Institute of America at San Diego. A member of the International Association of Egyptologists, he is also listed in the Directory of North American Egyptologists. He retired from industry and teaching (Southwestern College in Southern California), and now teaches travelers to understand the writing of ancient Egypt with this abbreviated method for direct translation of hieroglyphs into English.

The authors regularly conduct tours that are fun, yet highly educational and have been offered for university credit. Contact the publisher for information about upcoming tours in Egypt, Persia (Iran), Syria, Lebanon, and Jordan.

Photo Credits

Illustrations

Hieroglyphic font software: *Inscribe for Windows* by Saqqara Technology, Oxford, England.

The Gods of Egypt, pages 23, 24 by Joan L. Fellows

False Door in the Tomb of Idu, page 35, by Ronald E Fellows

Tombs of the Nobles, pages 81-85, Porter, B. & Moss, R., Oxford University Press

Maps: Valley of the Kings, page 71 Valley of the Queens, page 75 by Joan L. Fellows

Front cover and page 63 drawing by Daniel Loilett

Archaeologists Centimeter Scales

The National Park Service - Museum Management Program has designated the Archaeological Institute of America, San Diego Society as a source for the printing and distribution of plastic scales used to indicate object size in photographs. The National Park Service, archaeologists, universities, museums, and photographers throughout the world are now using these centimeter scales. The set of two scales includes one each 12x2cm and 19x3cm and features a new non-glare finish.

US $6.00/set

Foreign Orders
US $7.00/set
Postage included

Send your order with check or money order payable in US Funds to:
R.E. Fellows Publishing
2014 Siegle Drive
Lemon Grove, CA 91945 USA

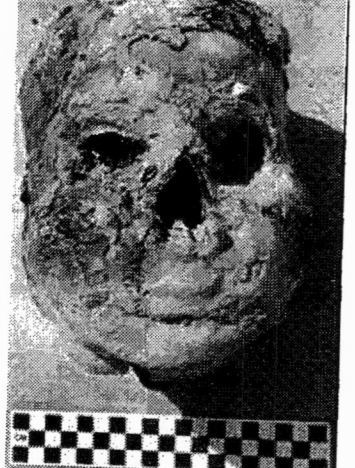

A mummy head from Theban Tomb 99, possibly Senneferi. Photo by Nigel Strudwick

---

Crescentic Stone

$6.00
the set

Archaeologists
Photographic Scales
© 1997 Archaeological Institute of America
San Diego Society
2014 Siegle Drive, Lemon Grove, CA 91945
Fax/Phone (619) 465-3841
As designed by The Museum Management Program
National Park Service

Spiekermann Travel Service
Your Middle East Experts
Visit Egypt, Jordan, Syria, Israel, Iran

- Private custom-made tour arrangements designed to fit your lifelong dream – and your budget.
- Group programs for Universities, Art Associations, Museums, Archaeological Societies, and others.

We include a personal touch: Sunset felucca parties on the Nile, performances of Whirling Dervishes, operas and concerts, and visits to an Egyptian home.

There's more: See the less frequented sites such as Dahshur, Faiyum, the Tombs of the Nobles, Desert Monasteries, the Western Oases, Nubian Museum, St. Simon Monastery, Dendera and Abydos Temples and much more.

Spiekermann Travel Service
31363 Harper Avenue, St Clair Shores, MI 48082
E-mail: goegypt@earthlink.net   Phones: 800-NILE-233 OR 810-415-9550
Visit our Web site: www.egyptinteractive.com/spiekermann/frameset.htm

Photo: Medinet Habu, sacred since the beginning of time